WOMEN AND SCHOOLING

ROSEMARY DEEM

Volume 70

Routledge
Taylor & Francis Group

LONDON AND NEW YORK

First published in 1978

This edition first published in 2012
by Routledge
2 Park Square, Milton Park, Abingdon, Oxfordshire OX14 4RN

Simultaneously published in the USA and Canada
by Routledge
711 Third Avenue, New York, NY 10017

First issued in paperback 2014

Routledge is an imprint of the Taylor and Francis Group, an informa company

British Library Cataloguing in Publication Data
A catalogue record for this book is available from the British Library

ISBN 13: 978-0-415-68357-9 (Volume 70)
ISBN 13: 978-0-415-75065-3 (pbk)

Publisher's Note
The publisher has gone to great lengths to ensure the quality of this reprint but
points out that some imperfections in the original copies may be apparent.

Disclaimer
The publisher has made every effort to trace copyright holders and would
welcome correspondence from those they have been unable to trace.

ROUTLEDGE REVIVALS: EDUCATION

WOMEN AND SCHOOLING

Women and Schooling

Rosemary Deem

Routledge & Kegan Paul
London, Henley and Boston

First published in 1978
by Routledge & Kegan Paul Ltd
39 Store Street,
London WC1E 7DD,
Broadway House,
Newtown Road,
Henley-on-Thames,
Oxon RG9 1EN and
9 Park Street,
Boston, Mass. 02108, USA
Set in IBM Press Roman
by Hope Services, Grove, Wantage,
and printed in Great Britain by
Lowe & Brydone Printers Ltd.,
Thetford, Norfolk

British Library Cataloguing in Publication Data

Deem, Rosemary
   Women and schooling. — (Routledge education books).
   1. Sex discrimination in education. — Great Britain
   2. Women teachers — Great Britain
   3. Sex discrimination in employment — Great Britain
   I. Title
   376'.941   LC2042   78-40558

ISBN 0 7100 8957 0
ISBN 0 7100 8958 9 Pbk.

This book is dedicated to all women in education, everywhere.

Contents

Tables

Tables

Acknowledgments

I should like to thank Professor John Eggleston for asking me to write this book, and for his help and advice whilst it was being written. Dr M. A. Cruickshank's comments on Chapter 1 were also of assistance. Members of the British Sociological Association's Women's Caucus and Sexual Divisions study group have provided an invaluable source of encouragement and support. Papers read at some of their meetings have proved extremely useful in formulating many of the ideas contained in the book. My students at North Staffordshire Polytechnic (especially the 1976–7 Sociology of Education option group) have also played their part in the development of arguments and clarification of issues relating to the education of women.

June Lee coped very competently with the typing of the manuscript at very short notice.

Finally, I should like to thank Roger Murphy, of the Associated Examining Board Research Unit, Aldershot, for permission to reproduce Table 3.3 on p. 68. This Table originally appeared in a paper given by him at the British Psychological Society's conference on 'Sex Role Stereotyping' in July 1977. Tables 3.1, 3.2, 3.4, 3.5, 4.1, 4.2, 4.3, 5.1, 5.2 and 5.3 are reproduced with the permission of the Controller of Her Majesty's Stationery Office.

Chapter 1

The Entry of Women into Mass Education in a Capitalist Society

The development of mass education in England and Wales since the beginning of the nineteenth century has been marked by three crucial divisions: social class, ability and sex. The first has been given extensive treatment by sociologists and educationalists, and has been of implicit concern to many other groups interested in education.[1] The second has been exhaustively researched by both psychologists and sociologists, and their investigations have been used to justify and to deplore differential educational provision on the basis of ability level.[2] The third division, sex, has been the subject of much less analysis. Certainly a Report published in 1923 noted that girls were more lethargic in their school performance than were boys, and more likely to take arts subjects, which required less effort than sciences or practical subjects.[3] Although subsequent official reports on education have dealt in passing with the difficulties of educating girls in both academic subjects and the domestic arts,[4] there have been relatively few attempts systematically to analyse the education experiences and performances of girls in comparison with those of boys. No great endeavour has been made to discover whether sexual divisions are as relevant to education as are class and ability divisions. Only in the 1960s and 1970s with the growth of a significantly sized Women's Liberation Movement in Britain,[5] and the progress of legislation relating to equal treatment of males and females in public life,[6] have sexual divisions in education come to be perceived as a problem of considerable significance.[7]

1

It will be argued in this book that sexual divisions, in the process of bringing up children within the family, and more especially in the formal education of children carried out by schools, are of crucial importance both to an understanding of the position of women in capitalist society, and to a comprehension of how the division of labour between the sexes is maintained.[8] Through their use of science and technology, capitalist societies have increased the mastery of human beings over the natural world, and over biological and physiological constraints on human behaviour and thought. In such societies, therefore, it might be expected that biological and physiological differences between individuals of different sexes would be of much less importance to the organization and relationships found in these societies, than in previous forms of society. In the latter instance, biological and other innate differences, such as muscular strength or the capacity to become pregnant, might have been expected to exercise greater influence over what tasks individuals of different sex carried out. But in most capitalist societies there remains a strongly entrenched sexual division of labour, separating what women do from what men do.[9] Because of this, it is both possible and feasible to argue that the sexual division of labour must be essential to the maintenance of capitalist society, although the exact ways in which it is important, particularly in relation to the family, remain controversial.[10]

Althusser has argued that societies involved in the production of goods must, in order to continue that production, reproduce both the forces of production (that is, in capitalist society, those who work for wages, technology and the means by which production is carried out) and the existing relationships of production.[11] The latter include relationships between workers and employers, relationships between social classes, and the sexual division of labour. Whereas the means of production are reproduced within the economic system by means of profits, labour power and the social relationships of production are reproduced by a number of institutions, including the family and the school. These institutions are called by Althusser Ideological State Apparatuses (ISAs), and they differ from other apparatuses of the state in capitalist societies in that their primary function is to pass on ideology, rather than to repress individuals through the use of violence, as does the police force or the army.[12] Ideology comprises not only ideas, but also the practices of different class groups.[13] Families pass on to children their own cultural beliefs and ideas, and also the styles of living and behaviour which they themselves use; Bourdieu calls this their 'cultural capital'.[14] In school, Althusser claims that children learn two main items: first, the techniques or 'know-how' of the dominant culture in society, and second, what he describes as the 'rules of good behaviour' which are 'rules of respect for the socio-technical division of labour and ultimately the rules of order established by class domination'.[15]

In the case of both boys and girls the techniques learnt usually include both literacy and numeracy, but it will be argued in a subsequent chapter that whereas boys are usually more than adequately socialized into numeracy (and into spatial and abstract thinking), girls are often effectively taught only skills of literacy. And whereas boys, according to whether they are the sons of capitalist employers, middle-class professionals, or working-class semi-skilled labourers, learn at school their appropriate place in the class and work hierarchy, girls, irrespective of their class background, are much more likely to learn that a woman's place and primary responsibilities lie in the *home* and the family, not in the labour market. Class variations in this, of course, occur; in the nineteenth century the daughters of the bourgeoisie who were educated learnt a very different culture (that of accomplishment in conversation, music and needlework, for example) from that learnt by working-class girls. Whereas most girls from the bourgeoisie were expected to supervise their servants, rather than carry out domestic labour or rear their children themselves, working-class girls were taught that their lives would be spent in doing domestic work, either in domestic service for others or for their own husbands and families.[16] Such class variations still occur; whereas working-class girls today are expected to give up altogether their unskilled or semi-skilled occupations after marriage or the birth of children, middle-class girls may be encouraged to combine a career with marriage.[17]

Hence it is argued that schools, together with the family, contribute heavily towards the maintenance of a society's social relationships of production, including class relationships

3

and the sexual division of labour. But for many girls, the school joined the family in this process much later than was the case for most boys, and the relationship between the church and family (which Althusser claims has been replaced by the school–family coupling), was also operative to a much greater extent for boys, who could take an active part in church activities, and for whom churches provided education long before they also provided education for girls. Whereas boys were considered an essential part of the church and, at the development of industrialization, of the labour force, and whereas those two factors played an important part in increasing educational facilities for boys, girls' roles in the church and in industrialization were considered to lie in the family, so that for them schooling was considered less necessary than for boys.[18] It was, indeed, only as the church, the state and charitable institutions began to realize that the sexual division of labour, morality and domestic skills could be taught more effectively in schools than in the family, that girls began to enter education in large numbers.

It is claimed, then, that there are strong connections between the subordinate position of women in capitalist society and the maintenance of that form of society, and that the maintenance of the sexual division of labour has, since the nineteenth century, been carried out increasingly by the school as well as the family. The relationship of capitalist employers to their employees is primarily an economic one, so that employers are more concerned with extracting profits from their businesses than with looking after the social welfare of their employees. The separation of work from home, and the nature of labour and work under capitalism has meant that the typical family unit has become the nuclear family, consisting of parents and immediate offspring not owning the means of production, and subsisting by selling labour power, not by home-based subsistence agriculture or craft-work. In order that wage labour may be kept healthy, well-fed and cared for, and reproduced in the form of new generations of children, women are expected to bear and rear children and to take the responsibility of caring for all members of their families outside of working hours. If women did not take some responsibility for tasks like child care, cooking, cleaning, washing and shopping, and if men had to share these tasks, then either employers would find their employees less healthy, or less hard-working, or with less time to work, or they and the state would be forced to provide many of the services which the nuclear family and women within it, now provide largely free of charge. A change such as this would radically alter the existing structure of society.

The expansion of education in the nineteenth century[19] owed as much to the demands of capitalist employers for a work force not entirely ignorant of the basic skills of literacy and numeracy, and to the church's belief that a limited amount of learning would enhance Christian beliefs — church worship and compliance with religious norms of behaviour — as to the efforts of liberal reformers who thought that everyone should be educated for its own sake. Capitalists, the church and charitable institutions all saw the education of girls in terms of the effects which it would have on their families (that is, in increasing their domestic skills so that a higher standard of care would be provided, and in raising the moral standards of their children and menfolk) rather than for the benefits which it might confer on girls themselves, and this has remained a dominant concept in the education of working-class girls to the present day.

Small Beginnings: Girls' Education 1800–70

Perhaps the most crucial difference between working-class girls and the daughters of the bourgeoisie lay in their actual, rather than in their ideologically-supposed, place in the sexual division of labour. There has grown up a myth that women, particularly married women, have only begun to participate in the labour market in large numbers during the twentieth century. But there is a great deal of evidence to show that working-class women formed a sizeable proportion of wage labour throughout the nineteenth century, and even before this time.[20] Furthermore, the Factory Acts which controlled the employment of women and children after the mid-nineteenth century would have been pointless if there were no women or children already being employed in productive work, and the Acts were evidence not just of a desire to protect women from the vagaries of industry, but in part expressed the ideology of the current sexual division of labour, which emphasized womens' place at home and in the family.[21] However, certainly not all women who worked in the nineteenth century were factory workers; some worked at home or laboured in small sweat-shop industries, and a very large number of working-class women were engaged in domestic service. By 1861 there were some 2½ million women (over one-quarter of the total female population) in paid employment, at a time when the benefits of contraception were almost unknown, so that a lengthy period in the lives of most women was devoted to child-bearing. Nearly half of the women employed were in domestic service,[22] a job which replicated many of the skills, characteristics and place in the sexual division of labour which most women were expected to take up anyway. For most married women in paid employment the extent to which they were financially better off was entirely dependent on their relationships with their husbands, although the 1857 Marriage and Divorce Act gave wives some financial rights and these were extended to include property rights by an Act of 1882.

Besides factory work, small industry, outwork and domestic service, some daughters of artisans and shopkeepers became governesses to private families, tutoring children in return for board, lodging and a tiny wage. Although the status of governesses exceeded that of ordinary domestic servants, the rewards and conditions of work were little different and, indeed, so many ex-governesses became destitute in their old age that in 1843 a Governesses' Benevolent Institution was set up to help them. Only a few girls from families of the bourgeoisie found their way into governessing. The majority of such girls were not expected by their families to work at all, but instead to devote their time to acquiring accomplishments which would make them attractive prospects on the marriage market, for as Borer (1976, p. 228) points out: 'Daughters were still regarded as the property of their parents, to be disposed of in marriage as they wished.' Once married, these women were not expected to engage in domestic labours themselves but merely to supervise their staff in the performance of domestic tasks, and otherwise to idle away their time in tea parties, musical evenings, sewing, embroidery, dancing and foreign conversation.

Girls from families of the bourgeoisie or the aristocracy were seldom educated outside the home before the last quarter of the nineteenth century, unlike their male peers who had enjoyed public and endowed school education well before this time. The Taunton Commission in 1868 found only twelve endowed schools for girls in the whole of England and thought little enough of the standards of these. Schools for middle- and upper-class girls were almost entirely single-sex establishments, whilst most working-class girls who were educated attended mixed schools. The question of single-sex versus co-educational schools in the education of girls is still a controversial issue.[23] While it is true that single-sex schools in the nineteenth century were able to place all their emphasis on learning which confirmed rather than challenged the existing class structure and sexual division of labour of society at that time, this was equally true of most mixed schools. Furthermore, some single-sex schools for the daughters of the bourgeoisie were pioneers in providing girls with an education which, while not confronting the sexual division of labour directly, did offer girls an education not radically dissimilar to that received by their male peers, and one which could provide them with the basis of an independent life style. Schools like the North London Collegiate and Queen's College, London were amongst the first to give girls the chance to learn 'masculine' subjects like maths and science. But on the other hand, the Taunton Commission in 1868, and the Public Schools Commission one hundred years later, both found fee-paying schools attended by girls to be of a lower academic standard than those establishments attended by boys.

By the middle of the nineteenth century there were in existence some colleges which trained intending teachers and offered a kind of secondary education to girls. These colleges had a very narrowly focused curriculum, and strong control was exercised over the behaviour of their students. For example, Sturt (1967, p. 155) quotes from the rules of a female college in York: 'No pupil to go without leave, nor write letters without permission. The envelopes of all letters to be signed by the superintendent or Miss C. Cruse.' Although male college students were often treated in a similar way,[24] there were different ideologies underlying the education of

7

the two sexes, with religious morality paramount in the college-training of many boys, but the sexual division of labour and conceptions of femininity influencing the college education of girls. There are also reports of mixed training establishments holding self and staff criticism sessions for men students, whilst the women students merely sat and listened.[25] Girls were often examined in subjects not taken by boys, such as seamstressing, knitting and sewing, whilst subjects like algebra, land surveying and geography were frequently reserved for boys. The cost of training female students was often less than the expenditure on male students, because the former required little equipment, and their learning of domestic skills could often be incorporated into the everyday running of the colleges themselves, thus reducing the number of domestic staff employed.

For working-class girls, their prospects of receiving any education at school or at home were much less than those of middle- and upper-class girls, and the content of working-class girls' education, when available, emphasized the domestic arts to a greater extent than the curriculum studied by middle-class girls. Accomplishments in singing, music or embroidery were not considered necessary for working-class girls. Before 1870, those working-class girls who were educated, whether in Sunday School, dame school, industrial school, or British or National School, received a basic curriculum which differed but little from that offered to working-class boys. But girls were likely to learn fewer arithmetical skills than boys — sometimes only those relevant to household budgeting — and no boys were forced to spend their afternoons engaged in needlework or knitting, although the crafts which boys did were equally related to their future class position and location in the division of labour. Since domestic service was the immediate fate of many girls on leaving school, and since their ultimate goal was held to be marriage and a family, emphasis was placed on providing instruction in skills and morality which would help girls to become obedient servants first, and subservient, thrifty and respectable housewives and mothers later. The possibility that girls would enter a different occupation, or fail to get married, was not considered. Anything out of the ordinary in school was usually reserved for boys, so that school outings, for instance, were rarely attended by girls. Turner, however, suggests that schools run by Quakers treated boys and girls more equally than did schools set up by other bodies.[26]

Once Kay-Shuttleworth became secretary of the Committee of Privy Council on Education, the state began to take an interest in education, giving money to some schools and setting up an Inspectorate to monitor standards, and the responsibility for preserving the class relations and sexual division of labour of the developing capitalist society began to pass slowly from church and private hands into those of the state. The passing of the first effective Factory Act concerning the employment of young children also increased the likelihood of working-class children receiving some education; children began to be seen less as tiny adults, and more as a separate group.[27] During the middle decades of the nineteenth century, children were often educated in single-room co-educational schools, but screens were used to divide boys from girls when the latter were engaged in activities such as needlework or sewing. Children taught in industrial schools often learnt little more than the simple skills they would need to work with, and those were usually carefully graded on the basis of sex. The 1862 Revised Code Regulations, which made grants to schools and payments to teachers dependent on the examination performance of their pupils, did little to widen the curriculum offered to either boys or girls in any type of school attended by working-class children.

It was not until after the 1867 Act which extended the franchise that pressure built up for a more satisfactory system of education to be made available to the working classes than the existing *ad hoc* arrangements. In the event, the 1870 Education Act did not prove to be the educational panacea of the working classes, which was hardly surprising since much of the enthusiasm for mass elementary education came from capitalist employers and professionals, who had much to gain from setting up a system of schooling which would minimally educate, impose morals upon and control working-class children so that they did not aspire beyond the social class or employment held by their parents. Even after the Act had been passed empowering locally elected school Boards, many areas, including large industrial cities, did not immediately provide sufficient schools for the children in their districts. Similarly, the 1869 Endowed Schools Act, which allowed endowments to be used to set up schools for girls as well as for boys, did not have a startling effect on the position of secondary education for middle-class girls. But the period after 1870 did see some significant changes in the educational chances of some middle-class girls, and also saw the increased involvement of the state in the education of the working class.

The Slow March of Mass Education for Girls: 1870–1901

The 1870 Education Act has sometimes been seen as a watershed in the history of the development of mass education. However, this view was not one held by its proponents or by many commentators and critics. Those concerned with the passage of the Bill through Parliament saw it as little more than a way of plugging the gaps in the existing voluntary system of education. Critics saw the legislation as evidence of the influence of capitalists in demanding a semi-literate but still subservient work force, which would be taught in inferior establishments by poorly trained, badly paid teachers. As well as requiring local School Boards to provide elementary schools in areas where existing voluntary provision was insufficient for the potential clientele, the Act also required parents to obtain instruction for their children, although compulsory education was not introduced in 1870; even after this was enacted in 1880, enforcement was sometimes difficult. Children sometimes failed to attend because they were already illegally engaged in wage labour, particularly in times of economic boom, and attendance was better in periods of economic recession when fewer jobs were available to children. Truancy amongst girls was less often because they were working for wages, but more frequently because they were required to look after young children and carry out domestic duties in households where all adult members were engaged in wage labour.[28] Furthermore, elementary education did not become even partially free until 1891, so that still other children failed to attend because their parents could not afford the fees, or were unable to clothe their children adequately enough to make school attendance possible.

10

For working-class girls then, the 1870 Act did not provide them with any solutions to their problems of being confined to low status work and domestic labour within the family, but indeed ensured that the structure of capitalist society which located men without capital in the labour market, and women without capital in domestic drudgery, continued to be reproduced. The education which working-class girls received in no way widened their horizons, for as Marks (1976, p. 190) points out:

> The philanthropic members of the middle classes . . .
> believed that if working class women could be educated
> to run their homes 'well', women would recreate the sacred
> middle-class resting place, and would thus discourage men
> from visiting public houses, and thus drunkenness, poverty
> and wife-beating would be stamped out. As a result, there
> were many schemes to include the domestic arts in the
> curricula of elementary schools.

Here, again, the ideology surrounding the utility of educating girls is clearly demonstrated to be in terms of the benefit to society, to capitalist production and to family life, rather than being seen to benefit girls themselves.

By 1876 domestic economy had become one of the subjects which earned grants for schools and was seen as a form of vocational training for girls, much as crafts or book-keeping might be seen as suitable vocational education for boys. That domestic economy also condemned many women to a life of public or private servitude was a proposition never considered, since the acceptance of the role of women in domestic labour was essential to the expansion of capitalist production. In 1882 cookery was added to the subjects which girls were encouraged to take at school because grants could be obtained for offering it. As Sharpe observes, girls at school were often only entered for one or two examinations which almost invariably included domestic economy, and the numbers taking this subject in elementary schools had risen from 3,307 in 1876 to 59,812 in 1882.[29] In 1890 laundry-work was also added to the elementary school curriculum. Thus, by the end of the nineteenth century sexual divisions in elementary education were clearly visible and the education of working-class girls was, if anything, more sex-specific than before 1870. While educational opportunities, albeit linked to the structure of the labour market and to class relationships, were beginning to expand for working-class boys, those available to girls were far less in extent. Lawson and Silver (1973, p. 341) state that: 'the education of working class girls . . . went side by side with that of boys, working class girls were not, however, promoted up the educational ladder in the same way as boys', but then, of course, there was no intention to do that, since girls were expected to take up quite different positions in the social relationships of production from their male peers.

During the period 1870 to 1901 middle-class girls did, it is true, fare rather better than their working-class sisters, and there is no doubt that their connections with the rising bourgeoisie class of capitalism were advantageous to them in this respect, although it is also true that male industrialists still sometimes tended to see their wives and daughters as possessions. Davies (1975, p. 39) points out that: 'Such men sought to express their wealth and developing power first through the finery and then through the idleness of their women.' But it is also important to remember that in the last quarter of the nineteenth century there were more women in the population of marriageable age than there were comparable men, so that some middle-class women were forced to find means of living independently, apart from a family. This period also saw the beginnings of the Suffragette Movement, and an expansion in the number and types of work available in the labour market. Although those three factors did not, in themselves, improve the standards of education offered, they increased the likelihood that middle-class girls would seek wider horizons than those offered by marriage, 'finery' and 'accomplishments'.

By 1870 girls were able to sit for both the Oxford and Cambridge local examinations, although only a few schools were able to give the necessary instruction and preparation for these. But doubts had been expressed about the suitability of competitive examinations for girls and, whereas boys sitting the examinations were given a merit ordering, girls were awarded only a pass or fail. And despite the passage in 1875 of legislation allowing universities to award degrees to women, and the opening of a college for women attached to

12

Cambridge, plus successful attempts by girls at the local examinations which qualified for university entrance, neither Oxford nor Cambridge awarded degrees to women until the twentieth century, and in Cambridge's case not until after the Second World War! Educated women were a threat to the established order, especially the sexual division of labour and the family, and it was constantly stated that women could do themselves irreparable damage if they engaged in intellectual pursuits, even rendering themselves unmarriageable.[30]

The 1869 Endowed Schools Act, together with pressure from those who felt the conditions experienced by governesses to be intolerable, succeeded in opening up more secondary education to girls, so that in 1895 the Bryce Commission on secondary education was able to say that there had probably been 'more change in the condition of secondary education for girls than in any other department of education'.[31] But although by then some girls' schools had begun to teach subjects like mathematics and science, other schools still presented to their female pupils a narrowly conceived education based on their class position, their place in the sexual division of labour, and on the cultural capital of the female members of their families. Whilst not subject to the stultifying round of domestic economy suffered by working-class girls, middle-class girls were taught arithmetic in relation to household budgeting, and spent more time engaged in music, singing and dancing lessons, riding, embroidery and foreign conversation than in learning sciences, technical or practical skills.

For those girls who did acquire a reasonable education, and who managed to escape from the clutches of their bourgeois parents, the structure of the labour market provided some possibility of independence and employment, albeit still within the confines of a rigid sexual division of labour. The creation of the County Boroughs and Counties, the reform of the Civil Service, changes in Post Office policy and the invention of the typewriter all brought jobs for clerks, telephonists and typists, many of whom were women. Teacher training was becoming more widely available and the opportunities in nursing were also greater. But if the expanding face of capitalism brought with it more jobs for women, these very jobs were to shape the future education that women received, and the flocking of women into such jobs marked the further extension of a dual labour market and sexually divided education system, both of which are still with us.[32]

The Commencement of Feminist Militancy and the Foundations of Mass Secondary Education: 1902–44

If the previous period saw changes in the position of middle-class girls and an improvement in their educational chances, the first four decades of the twentieth century also saw changes taking place in the education of working-class girls, and in their position in society.

During the early part of the century the Suffragette Movement rose to prominence, but it was undoubtedly a middle-class movement which had little or nothing to say to the ordinary working-class girl or woman. However, the strength of the suffragettes was proof of the success of at least some women in either educating themselves, or obtaining an education which to some extent transcended the traditional place of women in the sexual division of labour and allowed them to think in terms other than those of marriage, the family and domestic labour. But the attainment of partial female suffrage in 1918 was also attributable in no small measure to the long hours of work and effort expended by working-class women in maintaining the industrial production and sustaining the munitions industry of Britain whilst men were fighting in the First World War.[33] Neither the acquisition of full adult female suffrage in 1928, nor the growing political strength of the Labour Party had any significant impact on the ways in which working-class women were educated, since one cannot yet vote for a different curriculum, nor for a different sexual division of labour in society. Since 1928 relatively few women have become members of parliament, fewer still cabinet ministers, and almost none capitalist employers. It has taken almost half a century since full female adult suffrage to get legislation passed on the treatment of women at work and elsewhere, and that legislation has still to be proved effective.[34]

Since the end of the nineteenth century women from middle-class backgrounds – and to a lesser extent women of working-class origins – had begun to question their role in the sexual division of labour. The increased availability of contraceptives began to remove one of the biological props for the ideological and structural position of women as weak, subservient, child-bearing and child-rearing creatures. Although there was no real change in the percentage of women employed in wage labour between 1881 and 1951, with the figure remaining at just over a quarter of all females, there were almost certainly more women aware of the contradictions of having to carry out domestic labour within the family and at the same time engaging in wage labour. Family size began to decline among the middle classes first,[35] but Laslett estimates that family sizes for all classes reached their lowest levels during the Depression years of the 1930s.[36] Women who wanted to work or, as during the Depression, women who because of the nature of their work and low levels of pay could more easily obtain work than men, were more able to do so because the size of their families placed less of a burden upon them. The expansion of clerical and secretarial jobs, shopwork and the distributive trades, and the growth of the service sector, afforded job opportunities – albeit of an unsatisfactory and badly paid nature – to women of both the middle and working classes. The Sex Disqualification Removal Act of 1919 also opened the much-guarded male professions to women for the first time, although even now women are badly represented in many professions.

Within education itself changes still came, but slowly. The 1902 Education Act established Local Education Authorities to take charge of elementary education, although such education did not become free until the passage of the 1918 Education Act, and fees were not finally abolished until 1921. Like its predecessor, the 1870 Act, the 1902 Act was not conceived of in any belief that the working class had a right to education, but was much more closely linked to the economic demands of a capitalist system of commodity production. The education provided under the 1902 Act continued to emphasize to working-class children their class position, and their future role in the social relations of production. The Introduction to the 1904 School Code, which attempted to widen the curriculum for elementary schools, but which continued to include for girls the by now inevitable cookery, needlework and domestic skills, said:

15

The purpose of the Public Elementary Schools is to form and strengthen the character and to develop the intelligence of the children entrusted to it . . . assisting both girls and boys, according to their different needs, to fit themselves practically as well as intellectually, for the work of life . . . to implant in the children habits of industry, self-control, and . . . perseverance.

It goes almost without saying that the 'work of life' assumed for girls was still that of being housewives and mothers, and domestic subjects were held to be an important facet of this. Furthermore, until the First World War, domestic service remained a major occupation of employed women, so that this too required the learning of similar skills.

In 1907 the Free Place Regulations provided a means by which the brighter members of the working class in elementary schools might obtain a free secondary education. However, in the same year, maintenance grants for pupil-teachers were ended, and although these were replaced by bursaries for those intending to become secondary school teachers, this now involved waiting until the age of seventeen to enter a college training course, and a delay in earning a salary of several years, so that some working-class boys and girls were deterred from entering teaching. The proportion of unqualified to qualified teachers remained the same as at the beginning of the century, with one-half possessing no qualifications, but the advent of the Free Place system might, in other circumstances, have been expected to increase the numbers of members of the working class entering teaching as qualified teachers. By 1920 some 185,000 girls were receiving a free secondary education, and in 1921 the minimum age for leaving school was raised to fourteen years, so that all working-class children were able to stay on longer at school. But in 1933 the Free Places at secondary schools became Special Places and subject to a means test, so that some working-class children were prevented from benefiting from a secondary education. (Such schools gave a more advanced education than found in most of the elementary schools which other children, unable to pay fees, had to attend until leaving school.) The 1930s also saw the advent of intelligence-testing as a way of selecting which working-class children should receive a secondary education.

Although by the end of the First World War domestic service as an occupation had already begun to decline, long after this time schools continued to educate working-class girls for entry to this job as well as to prepare them to care for their own families later on. Alternative lifestyles to domestic labour were never given any consideration. By the 1930s some secondary schools even had special house-craft flats built in to their domestic science rooms, so that even at school girls could not escape being inextricably linked with the home and domestic work. A series of Official Reports on education preceded the passing of the 1944 Education Act and, for the most part, these proceeded to talk about educating boys, pausing only briefly to comment on the necessity to educate girls in child care and domestic skills. Thus, no chance was missed to emphasize to those responsible for educating girls that the paramount task of the schools here was to reinforce and reproduce the existing sexual division of labour. For example, the 1926 Hadow Report emphasized the importance of teaching girls housewifery if the nation was to enjoy future prosperity, thus illustrating clearly the dependence of a capitalist society on the continued performance of domestic labour by women. The 1943 Norwood Report on Curriculum and Examinations in Secondary Schools scarcely mentioned girls in its general sections, except in connection with general studies courses in the sixth form, and in commenting that girls found School Certificate maths more difficult than boys. Girls were singled out for special mention, however, in a section on domestic subjects, when it was declared by the Report that:[37]

> The grounds for including Domestic subjects in the curriculum are variously stated in the evidence submitted to us; briefly, they are, first that knowledge of such subjects is a necessary equipment for all girls as potential makers of homes.

Women who read that might be forgiven for thinking that the advent of free education for many girls had brought them nothing more than the opportunity to learn, in the formal environment of a school, all those domestic skills which they could, in former times, have learnt at home.

The period after 1902 was probably more successful with

regard to the education of middle-class girls. Although the standards of girls' secondary education still remained low in some schools, and in others the curriculum offered continued to emphasize only the liberal arts, changes outside education were influential inside education. The gradual expansion of employment opportunities, the Suffragette Movement, and the opening up of the professions and universities exerted pressure and demands on the secondary education of girls which had to be met by some, if not all, schools. However, this pressure was not seen by all as a healthy one and there was rising concern about the amount of strain which the taking of School Certificate Examinations might impose on girls, and Lowndes (1969, p. 92) comments that: 'the parents saw in three years strenuous preparation for the examinations a potent source of overstrain, particularly in the case of girls'. A Report in 1923 on the 'Differentiation of Curricula between the Sexes' also noted the strain imposed on girls by secondary education, remarking on the capacity of girls but not boys, to do work which they had been set even if it exhausted them. It does not seem to have occurred to anyone that one source of strain may have been the contradictory expectations which school, parents and capitalist society faced girls with, nor that the docility and subservience into which girls are socialized may predispose them to finish every task they are set without question or complaint.

The curriculum of middle-class girls' schools was not always noticeably wider than that found in elementary schools, or in secondary schools attended by working-class children with free or 'special' places. Few schools attended by middle-class girls had the necessary resources to teach sciences properly, other than biology, and when sciences were offered to girls, they were often presented in terms of explaining the working of domestic equipment or the principles of domestic tasks such as cooking.[38] Sciences were largely seen as 'masculine' subjects inappropriate to girls, since science and technology were mainly of use in the production of goods and profits, a world from which girls were largely excluded. Thus, schools in the early part of this century initiated something which has proved hard to eradicate — a tradition that sciences are not for girls.[39] After the beginning of the twentieth century, many more middle-class girls began to enter higher education. But the subjects which they studied were mainly arts, or social sciences which, in the pioneering days of the early twentieth century, were closely tied to careers in social work, and this pattern of subject choice still holds good today. By not teaching sciences to girls, or by teaching it at a different level and in a different context from the ways in which it is normally taught to boys, schools ensured then and ensure now, that girls are fixed in their positions in the sexual division of labour; whatever they go on to after school, whether higher education, further education or a job, they are excluded from whole areas of human knowledge, areas which could otherwise help them to break through at least some of the barriers of inequality erected by class relationships and the sexual division of labour.

Girls, Capitalism and Mass Education

Girls may have entered education in large numbers during the late nineteenth and early twentieth centuries but, on the whole, what they got out of that education was a confirmation of the position of women in the social relations of capitalism, particularly with regard to the sexual division of labour. The expansion of elementary education in England and Wales during the last part of the nineteenth century, and the early part of the twentieth century was closely tied to the interests of capitalism, and increasingly these interests were mediated by the state. It was not in the interests of the capitalist mode of production to encourage women to leave the home and the family for the labour market, except on a temporary basis in times of economic prosperity or in war time, since this would have meant finding alternative means of reproducing and rearing a replacement labour force and looking for other ways by which to ensure the welfare of wage labourers outside of work. Hence schools, whilst teaching girls some basic skills of literacy and numeracy in common with boys, at the same time constantly stressed the importance to girls of learning domestic skills which would enable them to become competent housewives, thrifty home-makers, and careful mothers. Whereas the education of boys, regardless of class position, was seen as something necessary for them as individuals (even if for working-class boys the ultimate benefactors were employers), the education of girls was perceived very differently. In educating girls, the main benefits were seen to accrue to homes and to families, and ultimately to the development of capitalism, not to girls themselves. This close link between the family, marriage and the education of girls is one which has remained strong until the present day.

As we shall see in the next chapter, the family itself is very important in the initial socialization of girls into ideologies about the sexual division of labour, and into a cultural capital which is at once isolating and home-centred, and vastly different from that passed on to boys. Education builds on what the family has already commenced, and in its reproduction of the sexual division of labour by different categorization and classification of girl pupils, their skills and qualifications (as opposed to the categorization and classification of boy pupils), points most girls in the direction of marriage and the family on leaving school. Education itself does not create the sexual division of labour, nor the kinds of work available in the labour market, nor the class relationships of society, but it rarely does anything to undermine these. Hence, although Adams (1975, p. 150) optimistically claims that: 'Just as the First World War resulted in women getting suffrage and the Sex Disqualification Removal Act, the Second one offered them equal education and equal pay', it will be demonstrated in this book that neither of the latter have really been achieved by women, and it will be suggested that the achievement of equal education by women is something incompatible with the present culture, ideology and social relationships of production in capitalist Britain.

Chapter 2

Sexism, Socialization and Culture in the Education of Girls

Culture and Education

It has been claimed that one of the two main aspects of learning in schools is the acquisition of the techniques and elements of culture.[1] Indeed the importance of the relationship between education and the dominant culture in a society has long been recognized.[2] Williams (1965, p. 195), for example, says that:

> the way in which education is organized can be seen to express, consciously and unconsciously, the wider organization of a culture and a society . . . the content of education . . . expresses . . . certain basic elements in the culture.

He goes on to emphasize that what comprises the content of education is a particular selection of knowledge, which is closely connected to the ways in which schooling and learning are organized.[3] Other writers have drawn attention to the fact that the kind of culture transmitted in schools is by no means always a culture shared by every group being educated,[4] and that this can adversely affect the educational experiences of those not sharing the culture being transmitted.[5]

In class societies, the family is an institution equal in importance to the school in the transmission of culture, which includes values, practices and beliefs as well as more tangible elements like literacy.[6] Cultural differences in capitalist societies are found between classes, with a marked variation between class groupings not owning the means of production,

21

and classes owning capital; but they are also found between the sexes. Class itself is an important factor influencing children's educational experiences; as Bernstein (1975, p. 28) comments:

> Class is a fundamental category of exclusion and this is reproduced in various ways in schools, through the social context and forms of transmission of education . . . working class children . . . are crucially disadvantaged.

But for girls, not only class but also their sex can help to exclude them from significant aspects of the educational experience. Because women in capitalist societies have a different and subordinate position in the division of labour compared with men, some of the knowledge, skills, values and ideas presented in schools are of no use to women, except as confirmation of their position in the sexual division of labour. Other aspects of the culture presented in schools serve merely to demonstrate to girls that their place in society is to rear children and carry out domestic labour. As Bourdieu (1973, p. 73) points out:

> the inheritance of cultural wealth which has been accumulated and bequeathed by previous generations only really belongs (although it is *theoretically* offered to everyone) to those endowed with the means of appropriating it for themselves.

In other words, schools may theoretically offer the same elements and techniques of culture to everyone, but dependent on their class position and their sex, they may or may not be able to make use of these aspects of culture. And schools have many subtle ways of indicating to children which aspects of culture they are supposed to absorb − and which they are not − whether by means of streaming pupils by ability, counselling subject choice on the basis of class, sex or ability, or in some other manner.[7]

Of course, it is possible to overstress the importance of cultural determination of human thought and action. As Stenhouse contends, if we see culture as the sole factor shaping the behaviour and thinking of individuals, and education as the main transmitter of culture, then education itself becomes nothing more than a process of indoctrination.[8] The dominant culture of a society rests on the economic, political and social organization of that society, and these also influence how people act and think. But even beyond this, individuals have some degree of choice, although cultural and structural factors may in some cases severely limit the extent of that choice. The problem is that it is usually much easier to do or to think as expected, rather than to choose an alternative way, particularly since the objective conditions of a society (for instance the limited number of well-paid rewarding jobs; the necessity for some people to care for children and carry out domestic labour) are likely to support what is culturally and ideologically expected, rather than what is deviant or nonconformist.[9] Some women, for example, do transcend the sexual division of labour, or successfully combine marriage and a career.[10] But most women are unable to challenge either the ideology or the structure of the sexual division of labour, and so much accept the cultural determination of their position in society (even if they are aware, or become aware, of the contradictions inherent in that sexual division of labour). Indeed, many of them are not even likely to perceive that position as having been determined, but rather as 'chosen'.

Sexism, Sex-stereotyping and Culture

The family, schools, culture and the structure of capitalist societies support each other to a remarkable degree in the process of subordinating and differentiating women on grounds of sex, and they do so often in very specific ways, although these are not necessarily visible to those on whom the process operates. Two concepts are frequently used to analyse the ways in which girls are socialized: sexism and sex-stereotyping. Sexism can best be understood as a process by which certain kinds of phenomena and behaviour are attributed to a particular sex. For example, Chafetz points out that in many Western societies the colour pink is associated with female, and the colour blue with male.[11] Crying, wearing skirts, horse-riding and washing-up are associated with being female, whilst 'keeping a stiff upper-lip', wearing trousers, playing football and mending cars are associated with being male. Yet there is no intrinsic quality about any of these actions or phenomena which demand that they be male or female. Scotsmen wear kilts, girls play football, boys ride horses, women mend cars and men wash up; but all of these actions may be seen as deviant or as 'unmasculine' or 'unfeminine' according to the sex of the individual concerned. Frazier and Sadker (1973, p. 2) go further in defining sexism and basing this on Shortridge's definition; they say it is:

A belief that the human sexes have a distinctive make-up that determines their respective lives, usually involving the idea that (1) one sex is superior and has the right to rule the other (2) a policy of enforcing such asserted right (3) a system of government and society based upon it.

It often used to be assumed that sexism applied only to women, and this definition reflects, whilst not requiring, such usage, but it should be made clear that in fact sexism can and does affect both men and women. For instance, textbooks used in school science teaching are sexist if their text and illustrations refer to and show only men.[12] Careers advice may be sexist if pupils interested in medicine are counselled to enter nursing if they are female, but advised to become doctors if they are male, regardless of personal preference or ability.[13]

The notion of sex-stereotyping is related to the concept of sexism, and refers to a process whereby individuals are social-ized into thinking that they have to act and think in a way appropriate to their sex. Sex-stereotyping is found in both formal education and in socialization processes, although there is no suggestion that *all* socialization and schooling con-sists of sex-stereotyping. However, girls who climb trees, play football and dislike wearing dresses, even if they are very young, are often labelled 'tomboys' by their parents and friends and encouraged to be more 'lady-like'. Similarly, boys who cry or play with dolls are warned that they are behaving 'like a little girl'. Personal inclination and interest are thus seen to be secondary to characterization on grounds of sex.

Sexism and sex-stereotyping are evident in the school curriculum in the way pupils interact with each other and with teachers, in reading schemes and textbooks, in the allo-cation and distribution of resources, in games and play facilities, in uniform and in many other aspects of education.[14] It is important to realize that sexism and sex-stereotyping are problematic not merely because they seek to constrain the thoughts and actions of individuals on grounds of sex, but because they frequently portray a picture of the real world which is inaccurate. As Lobban (1976, p. 42) says of her survey of sexism in reading schemes for young children'

> The world they depicted was not only sexist; it was more sexist than present reality and in many ways totally foreign to the majority of children, who do have . . . at least some experience of cross-sex activities.

Furthermore, sexism and sex-stereotyping can be extremely damaging to the self-images of those children who do not, cannot or do not wish to conform to the stereotypes. In her research on a comprehensive school Wolpe found that one boy who was unpopular with his classmates owed his unpopularity to the fact that he was seen as 'feminine'. This label was applied to him because he sometimes sat with the girls at lunchtime — an action considered taboo by all the other boys — disliked football and PE and preferred Beethoven to pop music. A girl who had few friends at school was interested in playing football, doing odd jobs around the house and disliked wearing pretty dresses.[15] Both children were thought by their classmates to be odd, because their preferred activities were those usually associated with the opposite sex. Their behaviour was seen by other children at school to threaten their own conformity to the stereotyped traditions of male and female behaviour.

It has, in fact, sometimes been argued that the high degree of continuity in sex roles in different societies over long periods of time is proof that sex roles have a strong biological basis and are thus difficult — or impossible — to alter.[16] But biological differences between men and women are not as straightforward as is sometimes claimed; the degree of biological distinguishability between the sexes can vary from a great deal to the almost imperceptible, so that the precise sex of some babies — or even adults — is sometimes in doubt and this may on occasions lead to individuals 'changing' their sex.[17] Furthermore, although biological differentiation between the sexes is based mainly on variations in the chromosome composition of cells which make up the human body, and on the possession or non-possession of certain hormones, we do not yet know enough about the effect of hormones on human behaviour to be able to say that biological factors in behaviour and thought are more basic (or less amenable to change) than cultural or psychological factors.[18]

In fact, sexism and sex-stereotyping of roles have been shown by many anthropological studies to vary in their context from one society to another, which suggests that cultural factors in behaviour and thought do override biological factors.[19] However, before examining in detail the ways in which sexism and sex-stereotyping work in socialization and schooling, it may be useful first to analyse briefly the ways in which girls and boys have been found – for whatever reason – to differ in abilities and attainment.

Sex Differences in Children

There is now quite a body of research in this area, some of it clearly displaying beliefs that sex differences illustrate the superiority of one sex over another. Early twentieth-century research by Thompson suggested that, whereas boys were superior in ingenuity, girls were better at association and at memorizing material.[20] Hollingsworth found that there were fewer 'feeble-minded' girls than boys but concluded that this was traceable to the less competitive nature of girls' work, which meant that mental disorders were harder to detect than they were in boys.[21] In a series of psychometric tests Terman and Miles discovered that there was a dichotomy of interests between boys and girls. Whereas boys had strong interests in exploits, adventure, out-door and physically strenuous activities, machinery, tools, science and inventions, girls preferred domestic affairs, aesthetic objects, sedentary and indoor activities, and looking after other people. Girls were revealed to have a marked superiority in verbal ability while boys were much better in mechanical ability. Terman and Miles also noted that whereas boys on the whole appeared self-assertive, aggressive and fearless, girls displayed greater powers of sympathy, were more timid and more apt to show emotion than were boys.[22]

26

More recent research has also discovered substantive differences between the sexes. Maccoby's review of this research provides a comprehensive account of contemporary research in this area.[23] There seems general agreement that, prior to attending school, the general intelligence of girls is higher than that of boys, but that after some time spent in school this position gradually reverses.[24] In verbal ability girls excel at the pre-school and early school stages, but by about the age of ten boys have almost caught up.[25] However, girls throughout their school careers are better at grammar, spelling and verbal fluency than boys.[26] Girls learn to count earlier than boys and, in the early years of schooling, few differences other than this are found in number ability between the sexes.[27] Later in their educational career boys start to forge ahead, especially in arithmetical ability.[28] In spatial ability, research suggests that from an early age boys are superior to girls and retain this advantage throughout the years of schooling.[29] Some tests for analytic ability show boys to be ahead of girls, but other tests show boys and girls with similar levels of ability.[30] Tests for creativity suggest that girls are better at what Hudson has termed 'divergent' thinking[31] which is often associated with creativity in the arts.[32] But other tests, for example those involving thinking of new ways to use toys, show boys as better creative thinkers.[33] Follow-up studies of exceptionally gifted children indicate that boys in this category are more likely to fulfil their promise than are girls.[34] There is also recognition in some research that girls are more passive than boys. Fogelman found that when children were given Piagetian tests of conservation of quantity, using Plasticine, girls performed better when they simply watched and commented on an experimenter, whereas boys performed better when they carried out the experiments themselves.[35]

Not only has it been established that there are differences in the skills and aptitudes acquired by boys and girls, but it has also been shown that these differences are reflected in school performance. Douglas (1967, pp. 99–100) states:[36]

There is much evidence from past studies that girls are more successful than boys in the primary schools. In reading, writing, English and spelling, the average eleven-year old girl beats the average eleven-year old boy. But although the girls retain their superiority in these basic subjects when they reach the secondary school, they fall behind the boys in many others, particularly arithmetic, geography and science.

Class differences may also overlay variations in performance according to sex, and Banks argues that the achievements of girls at school are even more dependent on class than those of boys.[37] Indeed, Douglas found that more girls than boys left school at the minimum age,[38] which is by no means surprising, since the opportunities available to working-class girls on leaving school (even more so than is the case for working-class boys) are rarely dependent on a high level of education or on educational qualifications gained at school. Yet at the age of transfer to secondary education, girls — regardless of class — are often rated as better educational prospects than boys.[39] And at the ages of eight and eleven years Douglas found that girls performed better in tests based on school subjects, although no clear sex differences emerged on the basis of IQ tests. However, he discovered that by the age of eleven middle-class boys were beginning to catch up, partly because of their performance in arithmetic tests. And whereas girls up to the age of eleven displayed better reading ability, boys were found to have a larger vocabulary.[40]

Once girls go on to secondary school their performance in relation to that of boys may begin to deteriorate, although Dale has claimed that this is more marked in girls attending single-sex schools than in girls at co-educational schools.[41] Douglas, Ross and Simpson found that at fifteen years of age, regardless of type of school, boys were surpassing girls in their school performance, with higher scores also on non-verbal intelligence tests, although girls continued to gain higher scores on verbal intelligence tests.[42] Other, more statistical data on the relative performances of boys and girls in GCE and CSE examinations confirm these findings on the relative performances of boys and girls at secondary school.[43] For the minority of girls who get as far as taking 'A' levels their achievements are not as good as those of comparable boys.[44] But, in any case, the majority of girls and boys at school are not highly academic, may not even take GCE 'O' level examinations, and certainly are unlikely to proceed to 'A' level courses. So we cannot assume that because the 'O' level achievements of those girls who sit these exams are broadly comparable to the results obtained by boys,[45] all girls do equally as well as all boys. Furthermore, girls at 'O' level tend to specialize mainly in arts subjects, whilst boys gravitate more towards maths and sciences, so that seemingly comparable exam results are frequently in quite different subjects.[46]

So far it has only been established that there are sex differences in aptitude, ability and performances. But it should not be assumed that these are innate or necessarily biologically rather than culturally influenced, especially since it has already been suggested that it is in the interest of a capitalist society to select different skills, values and ideas to transmit to different social groups.

Socialization into sex differences

Infancy and early childhood

The point at which sex differences begin to become apparent and the age at which boys and girls begin to be treated differently is the subject of some considerable debate. Chafetz, for example, argues that even the initial association of different colours with male or female babies has an impact on the ways in which parents and others act towards babies on the basis of their sex.[47] This view is shared by Goldberg and Lewis who, in their researches on very young infants, found that mothers of six-month-old baby girls talked to and touched them to a greater extent than was found to be the case for mothers of six-month-old baby boys. The same researchers also discovered that whereas mothers of male babies expected them to be noisy and adventurous, the mothers of female babies expected them to be quieter, cleaner and less venturesome than would have been required of boys.[48]

In contrast to these findings, the Newsons' study of infant care amongst families in Nottingham found few signs of differential treatment according to sex in the early years of children's lives, although they did note that some fathers were more willing to help care for a baby if it was male.[49] Their evidence does suggest, however, that if children are not stereotyped according to sex in early infancy, it is not long before sexism is visible to those children – whether or not they are aware of it. They comment that the roles played by working-class parents tend to be much more rigidly allocated on grounds of sex than those of middle-class parents, especially in relation to childcare and domestic labour, which are seen by many working-class men as 'women's work': 'it seems to be generally the case in our society that as one proceeds down the social scale, the sex roles become more sharply defined and more rigidly typed' (Newson and Newson, 1963, p. 207). The Newsons explained this finding by suggesting that as manual work relies to a greater extent on strength and muscle power than does non-manual work, working-class views on the biological basis of sex role differentiation are upheld by their work experiences. Although the extent of the difference in rigidity of sex role definition between working-class and middle-class parents may now be declining, rigid role definitions may continue to exist for those who are employed in heavy manual work, and be passed on to their children, so that the sexual division of labour comes to be seen by those children as having a firm biological – rather than social and economic – basis.

But children may at an early age learn the differential evaluation of sex roles even before they become aware of the biological basis of sex differences. Kohlberg's researches on five- and six-year-old children indicate that, by this age, children are not only aware of distinctions between male and female roles, but are also alert to society's higher valuation of men and male roles.[50]

Children of school-age

As children grow older, so their degree of awareness of sex differences and the extent of sex-stereotyped behaviour increases. The Newsons' work on seven-year-olds found many more variations in behaviour and parental response or attitudes based on sex than was visible at four years of age.[51] These findings are explained by the researchers by reference to the greater degree of autonomy which seven-year-old children have as compared with younger children. This reflects an implicit assumption by the Newsons that sex differences in behaviour are innate so that when children are allowed to choose their own activities they choose those which are in accordance with their membership of a particular sex. Other researchers have drawn rather different conclusions from similar evidence about sex differences in behaviour, suggesting that these are socially created rather than biologically based.[52] Chafetz (1974, p. 221), for example, argues that:

> Children learn from the actions of their parents and other adults with whom they come into contact. What we do with great effort and psychological cost to overcome sex role stereotypes will become our children's habitual responses

although this too is over-simplistic, since it assumes that sex stereotyping can be overcome simply by changing people's attitudes, without recognizing that the basic structure of capitalist societies is one in which the division of labour between the sexes plays a major part.

The actual differences in behaviour between boys and girls of primary school age may be quite striking. The Newsons found that mothers of seven-year-old boys were highly likely to characterize those boys as 'outdoor' children, whereas mothers of similarly aged girls most frequently described their daughters as children who spent a lot of time indoors.[53] That this should be the case might be expected from evidence examined earlier, which suggested that mothers of young boys were more likely to think of their sons as adventurous than were mothers of young girls.[54] And it was also established previously that mothers talk more to female babies than to male babies.[55] Hence, boys may well be encouraged to spend long periods of time outside, whilst girls are kept inside talking to their mothers, and gradually taking an interest in household domestic tasks. The boys in the Newsons' study who were said by their mothers to be 'indoor' children, were often considered to be shy, which explained (to their parents) their wish to stay indoors.[56] No such

31

characterization of 'indoor' girls was given, since staying inside was clearly felt by most parents to be normal behaviour for girls. The Newsons' researchers also showed that seven-year-old girls were much less likely than similarly aged boys to play in the street or roam outside. The mothers of these girls were more likely than mothers of boys in the study to fetch their children from school, suggesting that girls may be more closely supervised than boys.[57]

The skills and abilities in which children of different sexes excel or in which they are inferior at school, are reflected in the activities of those children when they are at home as well. The Newsons found that seven-year-old girls were much more likely than seven-year-old boys to list reading and writing among their special hobbies.[58] Making models, by comparison, was a hobby largely confined to boys, who were often introduced to it by their fathers; knitting and sewing were predominantly female pastimes.[59] Games and toys can also play an important role in stereotyping children's behaviour on the basis of sex.[60] The Newsons' research on these discovered that jigsaw puzzles were used mainly by middle-class boys, which may help to explain why boys do better on tests of spatial ability.[61] Both boys and girls were found to play ball games, but whereas boys preferred team games like cricket or football, girls preferred solitary games involving, for instance, the rhythmic bouncing of a ball on the ground. Lego and other constructional games were used mostly by boys, which may increase their mechanical ability as compared to girls. Dolls were an important toy for many girls, but few boys.[62] Although special dolls, such as Action Man, are made for boys, these are in a rather different category from most dolls played with by girls; they have no connection with the home, the family, appearance and domestic tasks as do most dolls played with by girls — indeed, Action Man may not even be classed as a doll. Girls' dolls — which are usually, although not always, female — encourage their owners to engage in traditional female behaviour — caring for others, playing 'Mummy', keeping house, sewing, showing concern for clothes and appearance — whereas boys' dolls are usually more adventurous male characters who can be used in 'masculine' play outside, as opposed to inside, the home. Belotti (1975, p. 80) questions whether girls' apparent preference for dolls — as opposed to other playthings — is a 'natural' preference:

> I have seen girls of eighteen or twenty months old spend hours and hours taking a whole lot of little cars, aeroplanes, helicopters, boats and trains from a bag, line them up on a carpet and move them about with the same pleasure and concentration as little boys. In the same way one can see boys spending the whole morning washing, cleaning the tables and polishing shoes. Later this pattern of play disappears. Children have already learnt to ask for the 'right' toy because they know the 'wrong' one will be denied them.

The Newsons argue that the play of girls tends to mirror that of adult women with whom they come into contact. Hence, their play involves looking after babies, doing housework, going shopping, visiting the doctor or going on holiday. This is claimed to be the case even where a girl's own mother works! If this is so, then there needs to be a more convincing explanation of why girls adopt domestic roles than the Newsons' suggestion that these roles are most easily accessible to and observable by girls. Boys, the Newsons suggest, cannot observe men's roles as easily (because they are all hidden away at work) and hence use more fantasy and creativity in their play.[63] But this may be made more possible for boys than for girls because television, radio, films and comics portray far more men in heroic and fantasy roles than they do women. Girls looking for alternative female roles are likely to be confronted in the media with yet more unheroic, housewifely figures whose fantasies are confined to dreaming about romance with the milkman or washing-machine mechanic. It is also likely that girls are encouraged by their mothers to engage in domestic duties, whilst boys are not so encouraged and, indeed, may even be discouraged from so doing. Thus, whilst girls are learning that domestic tasks are 'female work', boys are also learning this stereotype, which they will apply later to their own girlfriends and wives, and which is also supported by society's existing sexual division of labour.

At the same time, girls are also likely to be learning the appropriate 'female' manner in which to express emotion. The Newsons found that seven-year-old girls who quarrelled with their friends did so by shouting at them, whilst boys who argued with their friends were likely to settle disputes by the use of physical force.[64] They comment (1976, p. 198) that this is related to 'a cultural understanding that it is neither seemly nor safe to allow little girls to brawl in public places'. On the other hand, girls were reported by their mothers to display more aggression at home than boys, and the Newsons (1976, p. 198) explain this by declaring that 'the sanction [against aggression] is lifted in the privacy of the home to the extent that female aggression if not exactly accepted, is not totally forbidden'. The showing of aggression in public by girls may also be made less likely by other processes at work in their socialization. The Newsons discovered that mothers of girls were more likely to intervene when their daughters became involved in unsuitable friendships, than was the case for similarly involved boys. And because girls are less free to choose their friends and roam the streets, they are less likely to use bad language, or perhaps less likely to let their parents hear them use it. Girls may, because of their socialization, be easier to bring up; the Newsons' research found that girls were threatened with punishment and punished less often than boys,[65] and that few girls were considered by their parents to be difficult to handle, whilst boys were placed in this category quite frequently.[66]

The evidence on socialization so far examined suggests that, within the family and in the early years of schooling, boys and girls behave differently, acquire different skills and aptitudes, and are often treated by their families and other adults in sex-related ways. This supports the argument presented by Althusser that the family, in combination with the school, acts to reproduce and confirm the existing sexual division of labour in society.[67] Boys and girls quickly become aware of sex-role differences and begin to accept them as normal and 'given', so that what could be considered problematic is rarely seen as such. But it is not only with regard to activities, attitudes and skills that there are differences between the sexes. The consequences of different socialization processes based on sex are also to be seen in the cultures which pre-adolescent − and adolescent − girls typically adopt.

Girls and 'Feminine' Culture

The socialization of girls does not cease to become separate to that of boys at adolescence, but continues to differ as girls become teenagers. Yet, as McRobbie and Garber indicate, studies of youth culture have largely ignored girls, or perceived them as marginal to the sub-cultures studied.[68] However, McRobbie and Garber argue, the reason that girls are marginal to male youth cultures is because the culture of girls is often distinct from that of boys. Working-class girls usually have interests and pursuits different from working-class boys, and are much more home-based in their leisure time.[69] Middle-class girls may have more money to spend on leisure than working-class girls — at least until the latter start work — and hence may spend less time at home than their working-class sisters, particularly if they are involved in sports like riding, tennis or skating, or in hobbies like singing or ballet; but even so their culture is usually very different from that of middle-class boys. Smith comments that teenage girls may often be under greater pressure than teenage boys to carry out household tasks, and hence less likely to have considerable leisure time when not at school or doing homework. Spending money on clothes, hairdressing and cosmetics, he suggests, may form an important part of what leisure girls do enjoy; boys, on the other hand, although they may spend money on clothes, are less likely to be as concerned as girls with their appearance.[70] Much of the research on the culture of adolescent girls — and there is not nearly as much of this research as there is comparable research on boys — points out the greater home-centredness of girls' culture. As we saw earlier, even very young girls are encouraged and expected to stay at home much more than are boys, so this trend is merely continued into adolescence, by which time it has become an accepted part of 'being a girl'. Whereas middle-class girls in late adolescence may come into contact with student cultures and become more independent of the home, working-class girls are unlikely to undergo this experience. Some of the hobbies which girls take up, for example, cooking or sewing, may later form part of the blurring of leisure and work which is characteristic of the housewife's role, and the home-centredness of those hobbies may help to prepare

35

the girls concerned for the isolation which they will experience when they become housewives.[71]

What McRobbie and Garber term the 'Teeny Bopper' culture is ideally suited to girls who wish to stay at home during their leisure hours as it requires only a bedroom, record player and permission to invite girl friends to visit the house. Although teenage girls may go out with boys and spend much time thinking about them, there is much awareness that boys apply crude labels to girls who flaunt their sexuality or allow themselves to be sexually exploited. Furthermore, the 'Teeny Bopper' culture involves none of the risks of humiliation and degradation that may occur in the development of strong relationships with boys.[72] McRobbie and Garber (1976, p. 220) say:

> Involvement in Teeny Bopper culture, then, can be seen as a kind of defensive retreat away from the possibility of being sexually labelled, but also as displaying a high degree of self sufficiency within the various small female groupings; 'we have a great laugh with the girls'.

Boys, of course, may also engage in retreatist cultures not involving girls, for example in sports like rugby, or fishing, or in repairing cars and motorcycles. But these cultures are different from those of girls in that they are less often home-based and, where they are, often involve being in a garage, shed or garden rather than the house itself, which may be viewed solely as a place for the more domestic pursuits of girls and women. In so far as the 'Teeny Bopper' culture is oriented towards the idolizing of pop-stars, it is also claimed that it orients girls towards romance and anticipates future real relationships with boys, and eventually towards marriage itself – something which is viewed as an idyllic state.[73] In a subsequent paper McRobbie notes that many adolescent girls are aware that real marriages are not like this yet the fantasy of perfect marriage persists, partly because for many working-class girls with limited educational qualifications and few job skills, life presents few alternative ways of living as an adult. Furthermore, says McRobbie, girls are often aware that their leisure time and interests are boring and insular, but are unwilling to do anything to prevent this or develop new interests. Adolescence is seen as a time of waiting for real life – marriage

— to begin. But at the same time that very boredom and insularity are preparing girls for their future roles in the home.[74] Comics and magazines read by teenage girls are quite unlike those read by teenage boys. Whereas the latter tend to read magazines on specific topics, like football, motor cycles, cars or fishing, girls read magazines which talk about clothes, make-up, 'getting a man', and pop records or pop singers. Stories in girls' magazines are about love and romance, rather than about adventures, work or interesting activities.[75]

It is not only working-class girls, uninterested in school and doing badly there, who adopt home-centred cultures and are expressly concerned about pop music, boys, romance and clothes. Llewellyn, in her researches on two girls' secondary schools (one working-class, the other predominantly lower middle-class), found that teachers often complained that girls were uninterested in school work and only concerned with their social life. Indeed, at one school girls with steady boyfriends were seen as more stable and more likely to succeed in exams than girls without steady boyfriends.[76] Schools thus reinforce the separate culture of girls and in so doing help to reproduce the existing sexual division of labour, even where the girls concerned are academically capable. Llewellyn found that academically successful girls, especially working-class ones, tended to have a less active social life than other girls and spent less time 'hanging around' street corners near their homes.[77] But this may mean that even academically successful, lower middle-class girls are home-centred, unadventurous and passive.

Sharpe's analyses of schoolgirls in Ealing suggest that it is not only the Teeny Bopper culture which keeps girls at home, nor simply the need to undertake domestic tasks, but also the definite social control policies exercised by the parents or guardians of girls.[78] Adolescent girls are seen to be 'at risk' if they are allowed too much freedom. But even this practice is not without its problems, as Sharpe (1976, pp. 213–19) points out:

> Despite the so-called permissiveness of society today, girls are still kept under quite a strict family control, which has consequences beyond the simple one of their protection. Parents fear for the safety of their daughters if they are

out at night. But rather than equipping them with knowledge and confidence about the 'facts of life' many of them prefer a method of strict control.

For girls from immigrant families, particularly those emanating from cultures where marriages are arranged by parents for their daughters, control may be even stricter, so that immigrant girls may be prevented even from joining in the limited culture of English schoolgirls.[79] An Asian girl whose parents do allow her some freedom explains what it is like for some of her friends whose parents are stricter:[80]

> I have a lot of freedom by Indian standards. Some girls aren't allowed to go to school discos even when they finish at seven o'clock. If there is a school trip they have to take home a note from the teacher and even then their parents might not let them go. . . . Some of them aren't even allowed to take their friends home or go out for a walk.

Asian boys are given much more freedom than their sisters although, if their parents are very strict, they may have less freedom than comparable English boys.

The sub-cultures of pre-adolescent and adolescent girls are, then, usually quite separate from the sub-cultures of adolescent boys, or have only a marginal attachment to these. Girls' sub-cultures are frequently home-based, reflecting both their greater involvement in carrying out domestic chores, and their parents' desire to control them by keeping them at home. The cultures reflect — sometimes in a way closer to fantasy than to reality in detail (as opposed to outline) — the future roles of women in the sexual division of labour in society. Personal relationships, appearance, romance, marriage, and insularity, are the hall-marks of these cultures. And in school as well as in the family the ideological message which is passed on to the majority of girls is one which supports both the distinctive culture of their sex and the existing structure of capitalist society. It will be seen that this message is transmitted in a variety of ways.

Sexism in the School

1 *Pupil and teacher interaction*

Despite the recent interest shown by sociologists and educationalists in studies of classroom interaction[81] few of these studies have been explicitly concerned with the interaction of girls. Sometimes findings which contradict previous research have failed to be interpreted in terms which would account for the discrepancies: namely that the pupils concerned are girls.[82] Yet, given that the socialization and subcultures of girls differ, sometimes radically, from those of boys, it might be expected that the interaction of girls in school would differ from the interaction of boys in school.

The significance of girls' distinctive culture, however, is rarely recognized. For example Furlong's research which discovered fluid interaction amongst pupils, with children sometimes acting in groups and sometimes individually, in seeking an explanation of this phenomenon does not even mention that the pupils involved are female.[83] Yet we might expect that girls, who are encouraged to be much less competitive than boys, whose home-centred culture encourages self-sufficiency but at the same time the company of other girls, who are less involved in roaming the streets and in gang-formation than are boys, would display different patterns of classroom interaction from boys. This is apparent in the following extract from Furlong (1977, pp. 180–1):

Q. Why is history so good, what sort of things do you do?
Angela: Copying down notes from the board, writing notes from textbooks, and doing diagrams and things.
Q. Well some teachers run their classes by having discussions, do you think that's as good a way of learning as writing from the board?
Angela: No. I mean in your *spare* time you can discuss, but not in the lesson.

This girl's belief that good teaching and learning consists of writing down notes and copying things from the board – as opposed to discussing things and thinking them through – fits

39

remarkably well with Frazier and Sadker's (1973, p. 93) research which suggests that: 'Girls are reinforced for silence, for neatness and conformity – and in this dispensation of rewards, the process of learning is thwarted.' The reluctance of girls to participate in discussion is also characteristic of their performance in higher education.[84] And this despite their apparent superiority over boys in verbal ability. Here the sexism of the school seems to prevail over their potential aptitude for discussion.

Lambert's study of girls at school, which was a companion study to those done of boys in grammar and secondary modern schools by Lacey and Hargreaves, also shows findings which are rather different from those found by researchers in boys' schools.[85] Whereas Hargreaves found that deviant cliques of boys achieved poor academic performances in school, Lambert found that a somewhat similar grouping of girls was associated with reasonably good standards of academic work. The pressures to conform, to be neat, quiet and hardworking are obviously much greater and much more difficult to avoid for girls than they are for boys.

Delamont's research on an upper middle-class private girls' school does take into account the fact that the pupils concerned are female, but the relevance of her findings to this point is not always recognized, and in any case the girls studied are a quite atypical group in class terms.[86] Delamont discusses the role of youth culture in influencing school interaction, while failing to note that the cultures of girls differ markedly from those of boys. She also neglects to examine the impact of the distinctive socialization process undergone by girls, although the pupils studied seem to have almost an obsessive concern with being quiet, good at school work and getting teachers to like them. Their idea of a good pupil was that they should:[87]

Try to be good at the subject.
Always the right answer.
The better you are the better they are likely to like you,
but I think its basically liking the subject.

Boys seldom perceive their role in this way and there can be few boy pupils of whom it could be said, as it was of one girl in Delamont's study (1976, p. 70), that 'She only answers when she's sure she's right.' Indeed, Dale's research on single- and mixed-sex schools suggests that girls from single-sex schools like the one studied by Delamont are likely to have a more obsessive attitude to their work than girls from mixed schools, encouraged by the stricter discipline, absence of boys as a possible distraction and concern with academic work found in girls' only schools.[88]

Not only are girls in school encouraged to be silent, neat and conformist (as Frazier and Sadker show us),[89] they are also encouraged to play down their sexuality and yet at the same time to behave differently from boys. They are, therefore, frequently placed in a double bind situation; 'yes you are girls and must therefore be treated differently from boys', but 'you must not act or behave as girls normally do'. Wolpe in a study of a mixed school noticed that when girls complained about boys 'touching them up' on the corridors, neither the head teacher nor the other staff recognized the sexual connotations of the behaviour, which was teaching girls that they were sexually and socially passive objects to be manipulated by boys. The incidents were treated by teachers merely as indicative of boys' high spirits and of girls 'asking' to be interfered with.[90] Delamont in her examination of how teachers control pupils, notes that control of girls' dress may be an important strategy, with jewellery, make-up and other adornments being forbidden.[91] Boys may also be made to regulate their appearance, but looks are of far less importance to their sexuality than they are to the sexuality of girls.

Girls, then, interact with each other and their teachers in a way which frequently differs from the mode of interaction adopted by boys. But the sexism of school and school behaviour does not end here, but pervades the curriculum — and the hidden curriculum — which girls as pupils are offered.

2 Sexism in the curriculum

What exactly constitutes the curriculum of a school is the subject of some controversy; for example, it is sometimes understood simply as that which is officially taught in lessons. A broader definition is used by some educationalists[92] who conceptualize the curriculum as 'all the learning which is planned or guided by the school, whether it is carried on in groups or individually inside or outside the school'. Lawton (1975, p. 6) extends the definition of curriculum still further, by arguing that it is 'essentially a selection from the culture of a society', which is precisely the point which theorists like Bourdieu make about educational institutions when they contend that these institutions transmit the dominant culture of a society.[93] The problems which girls, particularly working-class girls, face with regard to the curriculum of a school include not only the fact that the selected culture is inappropriate to their own class position, practices and beliefs (a contradiction also faced by working-class boys), but also that the selected culture is inappropriate to their position in the sexual division of labour.

Sexism in the curriculum is something to which particular attention has been drawn both by the Women's Movement in Britain and also by the development of courses, mainly at post-school level, in Women's Studies.[94] These courses focus on women and women's interests, whether in literature, history, the arts, the social sciences or other areas of culture, and in so doing they and their compilers have made apparent the extent to which most subjects and areas of learning neglect the role of women and women's interests. History as taught in many schools, for example, deals mainly with the activities of men; literature is quite often concerned only or mostly with works written by men.

Where subjects or areas of learning do relate to women and women's interests, they often do so in a very restricted manner. For example, domestic science and needlework are considered to be 'feminine' subjects, but are concerned mainly with teaching girls how to be efficient housewives and mothers − not with instructing them in aesthetic or general skills − whilst at the same time boys may be discouraged from taking such subjects, as the skills involved are considered unnecessary for men.[95] Other subjects may have 'neutral' content in the sense that they relate to phenomena and skills which are not designed especially for either sex, but they may be taught in a sexist way with girls being encouraged not to take them, because they are 'masculine' subjects. Sciences, for example, particularly those like physics and chemistry, may use skills of numeracy and abstract thinking at which some girls are not particularly practised, and instead of trying to improve these skills so that girls can do well at sciences, some schools may try to move girls into other areas of learning.[96] Dale's research suggests that when girls do display an interest in the sciences, they are often most fascinated by those aspects dealing with people, rather than with the parts which concern the mechanics and explanation of non-human phenomena.[97]

A study of curricular differences between boys and girls at secondary schools carried out by a team of Her Majesty's School Inspectors found that many schools, whether unintentionally or deliberately, channel girls into separate areas of the curriculum from boys.[98] Girls may end up taking traditionally 'feminine' subjects like cookery, and also congregate in the arts disciplines, whilst boys gravitate towards practical, technical, mathematical and scientific subjects. In games and physical education boys and girls often undertake separate activities. The 'blocking' together of optional subjects often prevents pupils from mixing arts and sciences in the later years of secondary schooling.[99] Girls who want to study a science are often encouraged to take biology, a 'human interest' science dealing with animals and people; but on its own, without physics or chemistry, biology is of limited use (compared with other sciences) in gaining entry to higher and further education, or a job. Dale's work on mixed and single-sex schools claims that all pupils are likely to achieve a higher level of academic performance in co-educational rather than single-sex schools.[100] But other research indicates that, whether this is so or not, girls are more likely to choose maths and science subjects in single-sex schools than in co-educational schools, despite the fact that girls in co-educational schools are more likely to be offered the chance of taking sciences.[101]

Sharpe observes that girls may be discouraged from studying sciences because the teachers are frequently male, rather than female.[102] This may combine with girls' lack of experience or skill in the subject matter of sciences, and Sharpe says (1976, p. 148):

It is not surprising that many girls have relatively little interest in or understanding of, scientific or technical subjects. Their lack of experience of these at home, the absence in their characters of the independence associated with analytic abilities, and the apparent non-scientific nature of women's adult role also contributes to this.

Whilst boys appear to compensate for their relatively poorer reading performance and verbal skills by developing spatial, mechanical and analytic skills in the sciences and mathematics, girls seem frequently to capitalize on the verbal skills already acquired, without seriously attempting to develop or improve other skills. This helps to confine them to 'feminine' subjects and the arts.

Of course, some subjects which are not traditionally 'feminine' do take into account the role of women in society, and facilitate discussion on women's position in society; social sciences and social studies courses may provide an ideal vehicle for this. Yet in practice, these courses may do no more than examine women in relation to their traditional role within the family. This may have the effect of confirming women's existing position in society, rather than questioning it.[103] Even courses which do raise such questions may run into problems if they are given to pupils who have previously been taught in a sexist way. Griffiths found that when teaching a CSE Mode 3 course called 'Learning for Life' pupils were often reluctant to give up their traditional views on men and women in society and disliked thinking about the possibility of finding ways of living outside the nuclear family. Literature which approached problems in a non-sexist way was unpopular with her male students, who found such writing uninteresting. And because the course was seen by other teachers in the school as unconventional, discipline problems arising elsewhere amongst children taking the course were blamed on the course's 'subversive intentions'.[104]

Even seemingly innocuous courses, such as those dealing with sex education, may be taught in a sexist way. Davies has argued that some such courses see sexuality in females only in relation to love and the family while not treating male sexuality in this way at all. This view of women as different from men, and less free than them, is likely to confirm stereotypes rather than question them.[105]

Other courses are sexist in their content because they are

taken only, or mainly, by one sex. For example, most home economics is oriented towards girls, as is needlework. Technical drawing, woodwork and metalwork, are often oriented towards boys, although there are increasing numbers of schools which do try to ensure that everyone has a chance to take all kinds of practical and craft subjects. But just imagine the problems of a boy faced with these questions from a CSE 'Housecraft' paper:[106]

> Your brother and his friend are arriving home for breakfast after walking all night on a sponsored walk. Iron his shirt that you have previously washed, and press a pair of trousers ready for him to change into. Cook and serve a substantial breakfast for them, including toast. Lay the table ready for the meal. . . .
>
> Describe how to clean the following (i) a non-stick frying pan (ii) an ovenware glass casserole (iii) a thermoplastic (Marley) tiled floor (iv) a vinyl-covered floor (v) a lavatory pan.

Sexism in learning is much more apparent in secondary schooling than in primary schools. The Plowden Report found little evidence of girls and boys taking separate subjects at the primary level, except in games.[107] This, of course, does not preclude elements of sexism in the teaching of basic subjects like history, but because the range of subjects is smaller than in the secondary school, and because many primary schools place a strong emphasis on individual rather than class learning,[108] the extent of such sexism is probably much less than in the secondary school.

However, in one particular area of primary school learning, reading, much interest and concern has been shown about the extent of sexism (also class-bias and racism) found in reading schemes. Research has been carried out which pinpoints the elements of sexism in children's literature. It has been noted that reading schemes and books for young children rarely contain women as central characters.[109] Where they do, women are often portrayed as playing passive roles, as princesses or 'damsels in distress', or are helped and advised in their exploits by men. Less important female characters are most often described in domestic roles, engaging in tasks like cooking, washing up, ironing or cleaning floors, while menfolk look on. Men and boys usually have a more interesting time, even if they are shown within a family context, because they are able to go on outings, make models, take motor bikes and cars to pieces, never cook, wash-up or clean, and are the only people who drive cars. In her study of recent English reading schemes, Lobban (1976, p. 42) found hardly any working mothers in them, and a rigid distinction between masculine outdoor, instrumental activities and feminine, indoor, domestic activities.

> the reading schemes showed a 'real' world people by women and girls who were almost solely involved with domestic activity and whom the adventurous and innovative males might occasionally allow into their world (the rest of human activity and achievement) in a helpmate capacity.

Of course, it is arguable to what extent reading schemes do influence children's perceptions of the world, but since we do know that girls learn to read earlier than boys, it might be expected that any adverse effects would be felt more by girls than by boys. Certainly girls who have already been socialized into thinking that women's roles are rigidly separated from men's will have these beliefs confirmed by the sexist content of reading schemes. And for those girls who have different experiences of the roles of women to those portrayed, the reading schemes are likely to cause some bewilderment about what exactly society does expect of women.

In the curriculum then, sexism is apparent in a number of ways: it is present in the characterization of some subjects as male and some subjects as female; it is found in the content of some disciplines, which emphasize male rather than female endeavour, or which take for granted the existing position of women in society; and it is found in the orientation of subjects towards boys or girls. But learning itself is not the only aspect of schooling which is sexist. There is another and more subtle way in which education may be sexist, and that is in the 'hidden curriculum', in other words the 'invisible' manner in which learning is organized and shaped.

3 *Sexism in the hidden curriculum*

The emphasis placed by Marxist theorists on the functions of schooling in capitalist society in reproducing the social relations of production has caused attention to be directed not only at what children learn in school, but also at how they learn, that is the 'hidden' aspects of learning. Vallance (1974, p. 13) says:

> the functions of the hidden curriculum have been variously identified as the inculcation of values, political socialization, training in obedience and docility, the perpetuation of the class structure. . . . I use the term to refer to those non-academic but educationally significant consequences of schooling that occur systematically but are not made explicit at any level to the public rationales for education.

If aspects of the hidden curriculum are sexist, and indeed if schools are to reproduce the existing sexual division of labour, then it is likely that the hidden curriculum will be sexist so that, even if the curriculum itself becomes or is less explicit, pupils will continue to act and think in sex-stereotyped ways.

There are many aspects of the school and school day which incorporate some element of sexism. Adams and Laurikietis suggest a variety of means by which girls may be made to feel inferior to, or different from, boys.[110] Boys' names may be placed first on class registers, followed by girls' names. Female pupils may be lined up in separate rows from male pupils. In sports or in academic learning and examinations, girls may be urged to compete against boys and vice versa. In terms of uniform, girls are often required to wear restricting and impracticable skirts or gymslips, whilst only boys are allowed to wear trousers. School playgrounds are often segregated into areas for boys and areas for girls, with boys playing boisterous games on their section and girls behaving quietly on theirs. Describing one school where this is the case, Wolpe (1977, p. 39) points out that although the pupils had chosen to have segregated play areas, the girls' playground was thought to be boring because nothing exciting ever happened on it. She goes on to say:

> There are in fact no chances for girls to participate or to be physically active during the school breaks. Their own

quiet playground precludes this as all balls are banished from it. They cannot join in with the boys in football. The situation is structured in such a way that they have little alternative but to be onlookers. The game is a socially pre-scribed activity for boys.

This, of course, is encouraged by the rigid separation in many secondary schools of girls' games and PE from that of boys, something which often begins in primary schools. In assemblies girls may be allowed to sit whilst boys remain standing. Outings may be arranged separately for each sex.[111]

For children who attend mixed schools, the sex balance of the school staff may also reflect a separatist view of the capabilities of men and women, replicating the sexual division of labour in wider society. For instance, only a small number of heads of mixed comprehensive schools are women.[112] Most heads of sciences and maths departments are male, whilst there are more likely to be female heads of departments in subjects like English, history or languages, and most likely to be women heads of department in home economics or girls' games. Clerical and typing staff are almost certainly female in most schools, as are cleaners, cooks and meal supervisors; caretakers, on the other hand, who do 'heavy' work, will all be male. Conversely, however, children in primary schools may find quite a different situation, since teaching young children has long been regarded as womens' work — an extension of their 'caring' role from the home to the school.[113] Whereas being a headteacher or a head of department in a secondary school is seen to require authority and 'masculine' skills, these are not thought necessary in a primary school. Indeed, for many years one union of male teachers had as one of its objectives the achievement of a situation in which boys over the age of seven years should be taught only or mainly by men.[114] Sharpe suggests that one reason why boys do less well in primary school than they do in secondary school may be that primary school confronts them with a 'feminine' environment, not only in terms of the sex of the teachers, but also in terms of the behaviour which is required of them.[115] She says (1976, pp. 145-6):

In fact, the primary school values directly contradict the independent assertiveness that parents usually try to encourage in their sons. Although teachers may obtain some obedience and conformity from boys, it is likely that they see primary school as being a much more appropriate environment for girls. As a result boys have less incentive to work hard, and become more difficult to control.

Once children move on to a secondary school, women teachers may be seen by both girls and boys as less appropriate to the situation. Dale's study of mixed and single-sex schools gives some strong indications that this is frequently the case. Here are just three of the comments made by pupils in that research about women teachers:[116]

'Women teachers were not respected by the boys.'
'Boys did not like the mistresses telling them what to do and what not to do.'
'Women teachers are far more changeable in temperament than men. You know where you stand with men -- no bitchiness.'

Some boys in Dale's study felt that women teachers were unable to control their classes effectively and girls, particularly those from single-sex schools, felt that women were often harsh and unpleasant teachers. Dale's (1969, p. 175) own opinions about women teachers are made quite clear in his research:

it is generally acknowledged that the feminine mind takes great care of detail and if anything is over-conscientious (which leads to fussiness . . .). In the mixed school the men on the staff would keep such a process in check.

Dale's argument is that no secondary school should be single-sex or staffed by men or women only. The presence of male teachers makes women teachers less particular and stringent, and makes female pupils less silly and giggly and more co-operative. At the same time boys become less boisterous in the presence of girls.[117]

But what Dale sees as desirable staff–student relationships in a school may encompass exactly that sexism in behaviour which schools ought to be aiming to get away from, that is a belief that women should behave in a deferential and coquettish way towards men. As Wolpe notes in her study of a mixed secondary school, all that the presence of male teachers in a school may do is to teach girl pupils to behave in a traditionally stereotyped way, and reward them for so doing.[118] She cites one case where, in relation to a male teacher:[119]

> girls adopted a very 'coy' manner . . . when bringing up work to the desk or calling him over to discuss a particular aspect. 'Oh Sir', would be accompanied by a giggle, a fluttering of the eyes and a movement closer towards him. This type of behaviour did not occur in classes with older male teachers who distanced themselves from the children. . . .

There remains a suspicion then, that when Dale argues that male teachers modify the behaviour of female pupils and teachers, it is modification in terms of the traditional stereotypes of female behaviour in relation to men which he has in mind. But it is not only male teachers who help to create or confirm stereotyped behaviour, it is also sometimes encouraged by female teachers. Harrison, for example, suggests that female teachers may reinforce their female pupils' perceptions of themselves as pretty, submissive and unintellectual in relation to boys.[120]

Sexism may also operate unconsciously in the classroom by virtue of the degree of attention which teachers pay to male and female pupils. Frazier and Sadker argue that in a mixed class boys may often claim more of a teacher's attention than girls, because their behaviour is noisier and potentially more disruptive than that of girls.[121] Similar conclusions on the response of teachers to pupils of different sex have also been reached by Douglas and Griffiths.[122] The consequences of paying more attention to boys than girls may mean not only that boys take up more of their teachers' time and energy, whilst girls may be neglected, but may also result in girls failing to ask sufficient questions about their work and about the problems they encounter in that work, because they are used to working with less help from their teachers. Obviously not all teachers do spend more time teaching or disciplining male pupils than female pupils, and for some of those teachers who do, their action may be quite unintentional. Nevertheless, it is important to recognize that this kind of strategy is adopted by some teachers, and equally important to realize that it may have serious consequences for girls and boys in school, both in terms of understanding the work that they do and in relation to their own concepts of themselves as worthwhile pupils.

The connections between school and the economy and the labour market are, of course, crucial aspects of education in a capitalist industrial society, and the mechanisms whereby schools filter their pupils into jobs or impart ideas about appropriate jobs are often sexist, precisely because this is one way in which schools reproduce both the social relations of production and, more specifically, the sexual division of labour. Since the 'real' place of women in capitalist societies is in the family, any careers advice which girls receive at school is likely to be limited in extent, and frequently not taken seriously either by those offering it or those receiving it. The Sex Discrimination Act of 1975 has made blatant sexism in careers' literature illegal — for instance advising boys to become doctors but girls nurses — but the Act has probably had no impact on the verbal advice given to school-children, particularly since the structure of the labour market has not been significantly changed by the passage of legislation on sex discrimination. The more academically successful, middle-class schoolgirls are less likely to experience sexism in careers' advice than are working-class girls, since there is some provision for the former to enter the labour market in a serious way. Working-class girls, on the other hand, may be channelled into a narrow avenue of unskilled or temporary work. When doing research on two girls' secondary schools, Llewellyn once listened to a careers' talk given to secondary modern schoolgirls by a careers' adviser, in which the latter outlined two main criteria for choosing a job: whether a pupil shared a preference for liking people or things. Those who liked people were advised to enter shop or office work; those who preferred things were advised to seek jobs in factories.[123] Of course, many working-class boys have an equally limited choice of work, but that choice is determined mainly by their class position, and not by their sex. In a study of working-class schoolgirls Sharpe found that their career choices included jobs like office-work, teaching, nursing, shopwork, air hostessing, hairdressing and reception work.[124] She comments (1976), p. 164):

51

The jobs they chose reflected, of course, the jobs that were normally open to them; these, in turn, were usually extensions of their 'feminine' role and exploited some supposedly 'feminine' characteristics.

These 'feminine' characteristics included meeting new people, caring for others, looking well-groomed, and enjoyment of travel.

Of course, as Hussain points out, education itself is not entirely responsible for channelling individuals into occupations, since much of the selection of personnel is carried on outside of educational establishments, and educational qualifications are not, in themselves, entitlements to jobs, although they are important in determining access to jobs.[125] But careers' advice and the kind of qualifications acquired at school are relevant to the occupations which children decide to try to enter, and girls are often thus doubly disadvantaged. Employers, of course, do not want those who aspire to greater things than their class position and sex should allow. As a Training Officer in a retail store says:[126]

Our girls need to be able to read and write well, to add up, and to have the right manner. 'A' levels would simply give them ideas and make them restless.

There seems little difference between that kind of sentiment and the concern shown by nineteenth-century industrialists lest their employees should, by attending school, learn to think for themselves.

Sexism, Culture and Education: Some Conclusions

It has been suggested that, in capitalist societies, there are close connections between the family and the school in contributing to the maintenance and reproduction of those societies. Cultural differences exist between different classes, and these are first made apparent — and passed on — in the family. Schools subsequently transmit only a selection of culture, usually that of the dominant political and economic class in society. Some children, by virtue of their origin in the dominant class or because of their sex, are more able to make use of, and understand, the culture which is transmitted in schools. It is also clear, although most educational theorists ignore this point, that schools and families transmit different cultures to boys and to girls. These, sometimes quite radically different cultures, reflect the sexual division of labour in society as well as the class relationships. The socialization of girls and the cultures into which they become absorbed, frequently result in fairly rigid sex-stereotyping of skills and activities. At school these quickly make themselves apparent, with girls doing well at verbal skills and performing better at primary school than boys, but failing to develop satisfactory skill levels in spatial, mechanical or technical ability and often becoming less numerate than boys. The sexism of the curriculum, and the hidden curriculum, and the different patterns of interaction between female pupils and teachers (as compared with male pupils and teachers and particularly in the years of secondary schooling), combine to ensure that girls mainly specialize in different areas of learning from boys and that they are treated and seen in quite separate ways from male pupils. Thus, on leaving school, most girls are prepared only or mainly for the traditional place of women in the sexual division of labour: the home and the family.

The results of this process of establishing sex differences are entirely satisfactory for the capitalist labour market and society in general.[127] Workers are cared for by women, new potential workers are born and socialized within the family, and women are also available — either before or after marriage if economic necessity or culture dictates — for a variety of unskilled, low-paid, temporary or part-time jobs. The capitalist labour market has what Barron and Norris have called a 'dual' structure, where most well-paid, skilled, permanent full-time work is done by men, and other kinds of work mainly by women.[128]

Although it has been argued that family and school do, to a very large extent, ideologically reproduce both class relationships and the sexual division of labour, whilst transmitting only the culture of the dominant group in society, this is not necessarily to say that schools are unable to change at all unless the structure of capitalist society is altered first. Nor is it argued that every school, and every aspect of learning and its organization supports that capitalist society. Some schools are trying to overcome the worst aspects of sexism and sex-stereotyping in their curriculum, if not in their hidden curriculum. But this can only be successful if those involved in education believe that education is about fulfilling people's potential, and not about pleasing employers. And this is not an easy undertaking in a society where capital and profits finance most of the education provided for children, and at a time when educational expenditure is under heavy attack. However, as the next chapter will demonstrate, changes in education are necessary if women and men are ever to break away from the confines of the sexual division of labour. Education alone certainly cannot change the social relations of production, although for many years it was a firmly held belief that it could. But education may begin to alter people's attitudes towards the social relations of production and the sexual division of labour, however limited in extent that change of attitude may be, and it can begin to extend the range of skills which children learn at school. At the present time, however, the subtle sexism of socialization, culture, learning and the hidden curriculum, is heavily supported by the structure of capitalist society and this support is clearly reflected in the structuring of educational opportunities themselves.

Chapter 3

Patterns of Contemporary Curricular Discrimination and Differentiation in the Education of Girls

In the previous chapter it was suggested that the socialization, cultural forms and educational experiences of girls were pervaded by sexism and by processes of sex-stereotyping. But education in England and Wales has come a long way since the nineteenth century; every child of between five and sixteen years of age is now entitled to free primary and secondary schooling, and there is increased concern about the effects on educational performance of social class background and ability level. In particular the period since 1944 has seen many changes in the organization and content of education in England and Wales. The demise of the tripartite system of secondary education, including selective schools and the eleven-plus, is almost complete and grammar, technical and modern schools have in many areas been replaced by comprehensive secondary schools.[1] Reports have been issued dealing with all aspects of education ranging from primary schooling to higher education and giving consideration to equality of educational opportunity in relation to social class and ability.[2] Primary schools have moved towards a freer organization of learning and towards child-centred education, and secondary schools also have begun to experiment with different methods of teaching, used mixed ability teaching or new ways of streaming pupils, and expanded their curricula. An unprecedented expansion in higher education took place during the 1960s, both within the autonomous university sector and in the publicly controlled establishments. New public examinations for school leavers have been

55

introduced: the General Certificate of Education in 1951 and the Certificate of Secondary Education in 1963. The setting up of the Schools Council in 1964 to look at school curricula and the increased size of many comprehensive secondary schools have allowed and encouraged the widening of subject choice and curricular innovation. Much more recently concern has been shown about standards of literacy and numeracy in schools and the amount of control exercised by teachers over curriculum content, and a 'Great Debate' on education has taken place between politicians, civil servants, industrialists and parents.[3] A Sex Discrimination Act relating to education as well as to such matters as employment and the supply of goods, came into effect in December 1975, and an Equal Opportunities Commission was set up to deal with problems arising from the implementation of the Act, which makes discrimination on grounds of sex illegal in most areas of public life. Might we not now assume that girls, along with the working class and those of low academic ability, have finally achieved equality of opportunity?

The Concept of Equality

Since 1944 there has been much controversy in educational circles over the interpretation of the concept of equality, and particularly the concept of equality of educational opportunity. The 1944 Education Act itself saw equality as something which must be related to age, ability and aptitude. But the manner in which the Act was implemented ensured that these three factors merely served to determine which groups should have most resources, facilities and prestige, so that, for example, the secondary modern schools to which the vast majority of working-class children went were in no sense equal to the grammar schools attended by a small elite.[4] This preserved inequality, rather than decreasing its extent. In the decades since 1944 other definitions of equality of educational opportunity have also made themselves known, notably the idea of equal access to common secondary schools and the notion of compensatory education for particularly disadvantaged groups.[5] But contradictory principles of equality have made themselves manifest, so that whilst some seeking equality in education have seen its achievement as something to which everyone has a moral and ethical right, others have seen it in meritocratic terms — equality of access to elite positions on the basis of ability — rather than access based on wealth or inheritance. Finn and Grant have suggested that the notion of equality has provided the Labour Party, the political group most concerned with egalitarianism in education, with enormous problems because of the need the Party has felt to combine its endeavour to achieve equality with servicing of the economy.[6] At a time of economic recession, this contradiction is currently of considerable relevance to an understanding of what is happening both to the education of girls and to the education of the working class in general. At the same time that the strengthening of the economy is seen to be a major political priority, with consequent cuts in public expenditure and a shift of emphasis towards science and technology in educational resources and spending, there is also political concern about academic standards in schools, and about equality of opportunity for women. The two different trends in policy virtually cancel each other out, since rising unemployment, lack of educational expenditure and cut-backs in teacher training (all of which arise from current economic policy), effectively prevent the raising of academic standards in schools and block the achievement of equality of opportunity by women.

The notion of equality of opportunity in so far as it applies to education is, in any case, something which must be treated with caution. Certainly, during the 1950s and 1960s there was a belief prevalent among Labour Party politicians and members, and also amongst some educationalists, that changes in education could bring about changes in the inegalitarian structure of society as a whole. Thus, equalizing educational opportunity was seen as a way of equalizing the distribution of other kinds of opportunities and resources as well. However, since the 1960s it has become apparent that either the idea that eradication of educational inequality leads to eradication of societal inequality is mistaken or that the methods chosen to eradicate educational inequality have been unsuccessful.[7] Indeed, there seems an element of truth in both these conclusions. Eradication of unequal educational opportunities, even if this were possible to achieve, will not

by itself alter other aspects of societal inegalitarianism, particularly when the class relations and relations of production in
society remain unequal. The notion of equal opportunity
both supposes that children entering school are equal,
although for example a mass of evidence on working-class
children and their educational experiences indicates that
inequality is present before the age of entry to school,[8] and
implies that opportunities to become equal actually exist,
which in a class society and a system of production based on
a polarization between owners and non-owners of capital,
they manifestly do not.

The preceding chapter examined some of the processes
contributing to the inequality of girls in relation to boys. In
this chapter, it will be argued that developments in education
since 1944 have altered, but not eliminated, the extent to
which schools discriminate and differentiate between pupils
on the basis of their sex, and that consequently, despite the
concern to achieve equality of educational opportunity
shown by educationalists and policy-makers since the Second
World War, the educational chances and experiences of girls
continue to be different, and separate, from those of boys.

Developments in the Education of Girls since 1944

The immediate effects of the 1944 Education Act were beneficial to both working-class boys and working-class girls, since
the Act enabled them to obtain a secondary education as well
as an elementary one without the payment of fees or passing
of a scholarship examination. However, right up until the
1970s the leaving age was to remain a barrier to working-class
educational success. Although the leaving age was raised to
fifteen in 1947, the GCE examinations, which were established
in 1951, could only be taken by grammar school pupils at the
age of sixteen and by pupils at other schools at the age of
seventeen, and this remained the case until the Beloe Report
at the end of the decade recommended that these restrictions
should end. So until that time not only did many working-
class children at secondary modern schools lose the chance of
gaining GCE qualifications but, as the Gurney-Dixon Report
on early leaving noted, so did many working-class children at

grammar school, because they left school at the minimum age. Regardless of ability level, more working-class girls left grammar school early than did boys[9] and it is likely that one important reason for this was the belief that the education of a girl, who would almost certainly marry, was of less importance than the education of a boy, who would have to work for most of his life.

The Norwood Report which preceded the 1944 Act had indeed argued that the educational needs of children would vary according to their aptitude and their interests. Whilst the Report recognized that the particular interest of boys lay in their future jobs and careers, it claimed that the special interests of girls related mainly to their future roles as wives and mothers.[10] The Report failed to take into account both the possibility that some girls would not marry or would combine work with marriage, and the future roles of boys as husbands and fathers. And except in relation to domestic subjects, Norwood's discussion of curriculum implicitly assumed that the main object of its concern was the education of boys, an assumption which subsequent official Reports have also been guilty of making.

The Crowther Report *15–18* published in 1959 claimed to be concerned equally with both boys and girls[11] and appreciated that many girls would remain in paid employment even after marriage. Nevertheless, Crowther paid more attention to the academically able girl, who it was assumed would subsequently take up a dual role as worker and wife/mother, than to the less-able, working-class girl whose future was assumed to be likely to take a different form and towards whom (Crowther, 1959, p. 34):

> all schools can and should make adjustments . . . to the
> fact that marriage now looms much larger and nearer in
> the pupils' eyes than it ever has before . . . there is a clear
> case for a curriculum which respects the different roles
> they (i.e. boys and girls) play.

Despite this, the Report paid far more attention to girls and their future roles in marriage than to boys and their future roles in marriage. However, Crowther was one of the first Reports to recognize that some girls at least would find themselves playing a dual role as workers and wives, and it was also notable for the consideration given to the importance of girls continuing their education after leaving school. It is clear from the evidence presented by the Crowther Report that the specialization by girls in a narrow range of arts subjects in the later years of secondary schooling was something established in the early stages of secondary education for all. The Report also noted another trend which continues to affect the educational and occupational prospects of girls, that of entering secretarial, commercial or other further education courses of limited educational value after leaving school, and the failure of more than a very small percentage of girls to obtain day-release training from jobs which they entered before the age of eighteen.

The Newsom Report on the education of average and below-average ability students, like Crowther four years before, implicitly and explicitly recognized that changes were taking place in the status and employment prospects of girls. But this Report too felt obliged to emphasize once again that (Newsom, 1963, p. 37)

> For all girls, too, there is a group of interests relating to what many, perhaps most of them, would regard as their most important vocational concern, marriage . . . many girls are ready to respond to work relating to the wider aspects of home-making and family life and the care and upbringing of children.

The Report itself placed great stress on the necessity for school learning for girls to relate to their future family responsibilities and to their interests in personal appearance, dress and social behaviour.[12] Once again, the role of boys in marriage and domestic labour was neglected, as were any purely occupational interests which girls might have outside marriage, motherhood and personal relationships. Girls, indeed, were seen by the Report as being intellectually and emotionally different from boys, interested in subjects only if they related to people, caring for or relationships with others. In science, for instance (Newsom, 1963, p. 142):

> A boy is usually excited by the prospect of a science course. . . . He experiences a sense of wonder and a sense of power. The growth of wheat, the birth of a lamb, the

movement of clouds put him in awe of nature; the loco-
motive he sees as man's response; the switch and the
throttle are his magic wands. . . . The girl may come to the
science lesson with a less eager curiosity than the boy but
she too will need to feel at home with machinery.

It is hard to believe that there is really *so* much difference between the sexes: with every boy displaying a great curiosity
about the world, and every girl showing a total lack of
interest in it. The Newsom Report dealt only with children of
average or below-average ability and as in the Crowther
Report before it, there is an acceptance of the traditional
roles of marriage, family and domestic labour for the working-
class girl, although a transition to a dual role is recognized for
her middle-class sister. Thus is the insularity and home-
centredness of the culture of working-class girls reinforced.

The Robbins Report on Higher Education was published in
1963, the same year as Newsom, and it noted the lower percentage of girls as compared to boys entering higher education in Britain.[13] In 1962 only 7.3 per cent of the relevant
female age group, but 9.8 per cent of the appropriate male
age group obtained places in higher education. The Report
commented that (Robbins, 1963, p. 62):

rising professional requirements may in future lead to
more girls entering those occupations by means of full-
time courses in higher education.

Like Crowther, the Report noted with concern the tendency
for girls to specialize in arts subjects rather than in sciences.
In 1960–2 in England and Wales girls accounted for 66 per
cent of 'A' level arts-only passes but only 41 per cent of
science-only 'A' level passes. In addition, it was observed that
the 'A' level performances of girls did not match their performance at 'O' level. Only 6 girls to every 10 boys passed
two or more 'A' levels in England and Wales in 1962–3. This
was reflected too, said the Report, in the different higher
education destinations of the two sexes, with girls making up
only one-quarter of university students but two-thirds of
training college students. Girls were seen to be failing to enter
many professional occupations, despite having comparable
academic ability to boys, and this was attributed partly to
their failure to take science subjects (Robbins, 1963, p. 127):

it is desirable to encourage more girls to read applied science. At present, very few girls in this country seem to be attracted to a career in applied science and the contrast with some other countries, notably the Soviet Union, is very striking.

This Report at least recognized that there was nothing inherent in girls' biological make-up preventing them from reading sciences, which is in contradistinction to the stand taken on girls and science by Newsom. But as with Crowther, the main thrust of the Robbins Report was towards middle-class girls of high ability, a group seen to differ in many respects from working-class girls of lesser academic ability.

The Plowden Report on primary schooling in 1967 examined the differential school performances of boys and girls at pre-secondary level, noting the superiority of seven-year-old girls in reading and other verbal skills.[14] On the question of curriculum, the Report observed merely that (Plowden Report, 1967, p. 249)

the distinction between what is done by boys and girls has partly disappeared. Except possibly for the oldest children, it is quite artificial and unhelpful; boys enjoy stitchery and girls can benefit from work in wood and metal.

Plowden may also, unwittingly, have influenced the education of girls by encouraging the freeing of primary school teaching from rigid time-tabling and curricula, and the placing of emphasis on child-centred learning at an individual pace. This may either have decreased the tendency noted by Douglas for boys to gain more attention from teachers than girls, or alternatively, it may have increased this tendency.[15]

The development of comprehensive secondary schooling has progressed considerably since 1965 and the first attempt by a Labour Government to persuade Local Education Authorities to adopt this kind of schooling. Furthermore, in 1972 the school leaving age was raised to sixteen. By 1975 some 75 per cent of secondary school children were no longer undergoing any form of selection for entry into secondary education.[16] A wider range of curricula has become available to many children in state schools. Comprehensive schools have explicitly been seen by many of their protagonists as a way of ending class and ability distinctions in education, distinctions which by the early 1960s were seen by the Labour Party as compounding class inequalities in Britain. A former leader of the Labour Party, Harold Wilson, told the 1963 Party Conference that:[17]

> to train the scientists we are going to need will mean a revolution in our attitude to education . . . we believe in equality of opportunity . . . we simply cannot as a nation afford to neglect the educational development of a *single boy or girl*, we cannot afford to cut off three quarters or more of our children from virtually any chance of higher education [my italics].

The contradiction between the concept of equality and the need to service the economy mentioned in the earlier discussion of equality in this chapter, is also visible in this speech, nevertheless Wilson does explicitly refer to girls as well as to boys, without any of the implicit assumptions made by many official reports that only middle-class girls will need occupational training and a worthwhile education outside of domestic skills. It might, therefore, be reasonable to expect that, with the advent of comprehensive schooling, girls have indeed obtained this chance.

However, in their report on comprehensive schooling published in 1970, Benn and Simon found that at least 50 per cent of the schools they examined restricted some subjects to boys only and that 49 per cent of those schools also limited some subjects to girls only.[18] In the mid-1970s, with many more children attending comprehensive schools than when the Benn and Simon study was carried out, and with less than one-third of state secondary schools retaining single-sex status, some 98 per cent of mixed secondary schools continue to separate girls from boys at some point before their pupils are sixteen years old.[19] This applies even in crafts subjects, since not all schools operate a rotating system of craft education, so that all pupils have the opportunity to try out different crafts regardless of sex. Girls on non-examination, final-year ROSLA courses often have fewer choices of pre-vocational courses than boys.[20]

A recent DES Survey on Curricular Differences for boys and girls found that formal differences in curriculum between the sexes begin to crystallize from the age of seven years onwards, often starting with boys' crafts and games, and girls' crafts and games.[21] This was found to be the case also in middle schools, with greater differentiation commencing at entry to secondary schooling, although some schools claimed this to be the unintentional consequence of time-tabling problems or shortage of facilities. By the fourth and fifth years of secondary school most pupils were found to be experiencing a core curriculum of subjects like English, religious education, maths and PE, and a range of other optional subjects. Whilst noting that option choice might be made for a variety of reasons, the Report suggested that the structuring of option choices might also be responsible for influencing their shape. Over one-quarter of schools studied, for example, provided pre-emptive curriculum choices (DES Education Survey 21, 1975, p. 7):

> For example crafts' departments often will accept for technical drawing — a supposedly free choice subject — only those pupils who have already done metal-work, a subject from which girls are excluded.

A further 28 per cent of mixed schools in the research had option choices which encouraged early specialization in either arts or sciences by blocking certain subjects together. The Survey appraising its findings said (DES Education Survey 21, 1975, p. 21). 'there are significant differences in subjects studied by girls and by boys and these differences are too striking to be accepted without question'. Thus the tendency for girls to specialize in the arts and boys in the sciences noted by Crowther in the 1950s and Robbins in the 1960s is still with us in the 1970s and, as the DES Survey suggests, this trend is still marked enough to be worthy of further analysis.

Arts and Sciences in Curriculum Choice: Trends and Implications

The DES Survey on curricular differences does point out that different choices by girls and boys may reflect a variety of factors which have nothing to do with discrimination against one sex or the other: the influence of particular patternings of options, friends, families, teachers, and personal likes and dislikes. But these in themselves, as shown in chapter two, are also likely to be strongly affected by the differential socialization of girls and boys. And certainly a clear pattern of curricular differentiation does appear between boys and girls, and is important not only within schools, but also for post-school education and occupational choice, where a narrow or inappropriate range of specialist subjects may severely restrict further opportunities. Further, as Shaw (1976, p. 134) has noted:

> divisions of knowledge in their institutionalized form of curricula, correspond more or less directly to divisions of labour. We can see in the range of choice offered to boys and girls both the means and expression of economic and social control.

And social class differences may also affect the kinds of option choices made, with middle-class children being more aware of the implications of their choice; as Woods (1976, p. 197) points out:

> to the initiated middle class pupil it is his [*sic*] choice and he makes it carefully with a view to job, ability and prospects. To the estranged, generally working class pupil it is a line of least resistance.

Thus the working-class girl may be particularly vulnerable to pressures by others to choose subjects which will fit in with her expected future vocation as a wife and mother, rather than being as aware as some middle-class girls may be, that she is likely at some point to want, or need, interesting work outside the home.

If we ignore for the moment subject specialization in public examinations and look at the relative percentages of boys and girls in secondary schools who actually attempt CSE and GCE examinations, girls are actually more likely to be entered for CSE and GCE 'O' level examinations than are boys (see Table 3.1). A higher percentage of boys than girls leave school without having attempted any exams, and slightly more boys than girls leave school with no examination passes — despite having sat for examinations. Although a higher percentage of girls than boys obtain GCE 'O' level passes, this

TABLE 3.1 *School examination attempts and passes, all school leavers 1973–4*

%	Boys	Girls	All
Attempting no exam	20.00	18.20	19.20
Attempting exams, but no passes	2.10	1.70	1.90
Attempting CSE	61.50	64.70	62.90
Passing CSE in one or more subjects, Grade			
5 or above but no 'O' level passes	30.70	29.70	30.20
Attempting GCE 'O' levels	47.20	50.10	48.60
Passing 1–4 'O' levels but no 'A' level passes	23.10	25.80	24.40
Passing 5 or more 'O' levels, but no 'A'			
level passes	7.70	10.00	8.90
Attempting GCE 'A' levels	18.60	16.90	17.80
Passing 1 'A' level	3.10	3.50	3.30
Passing 2 'A' levels	4.10	4.40	4.30
Passing 3 'A' levels	9.20	6.60	7.90

Source: DES Statistics of Education 1974, vol. 2, *School Leavers*, Table D, p. 5.

position is reversed in CSE examination passes. At 'A' level, a higher percentage of boys than girls sit the examinations. Girls have a better record in passing one or two subjects at 'A' level, but boys are more successful in obtaining three or more 'A' level passes.

Within these patterns of examination attempts and passes, however, another trend is also clearly visible. This is the tendency already noted for girls to take mainly arts subjects, and for boys to specialize to a greater extent in mathematical, scientific and technical disciplines. In Table 3.2 can be seen the distribution of passes and subjects for boys and girls sitting CSE examinations in the summer of 1970 and 1974. In English and history there are broadly similar numbers of passes between boys and girls. But far more girls are successful in French than boys, whereas this pattern is slightly reversed for maths and to a much greater extent for physics. Whereas in biology there are twice as many passes by girls as by boys, few girls obtain passes in technical drawing or metal or woodwork. Boys and girls do about the same in social

TABLE 3.2 *CSE Examination passes 1970 and 1974 (Grade 5 or better), selected subjects*

Subject	1970		1974	
	Boys	Girls	Boys	Girls
English	95,855	84,551	185,562	191,275
History	36,281	32,954	59,328	60,562
French	20,790	30,587	37,127	59,492
Maths	89,582	76,294	152,672	142,801
Physics	46,180	4,181	76,074	10,221
Biology	14,558	36,576	35,261	78,465
Technical drawing	47,356	358	69,418	860
Metalwork and woodwork	52,027	96	92,015	533
Geography	49,165	33,303	80,043	58,980
Domestic subjects	1,111	54,653	5,524	109,787
Commercial	5,609	27,318	10,031	50,231
Social sciences and vocational	9,326	8,972	35,438	38,384

Source: DES Statistics of Education 1974, vol. 2, *School Leavers*, Table 33, p. 70.

science and vocational subjects, but boys score greater successes in geography, whilst rarely obtaining passes in commercial or domestic subjects, both of which are taken and passed by girls in large numbers.

Similar patterns of subject choice are also apparent at GCE 'O' level where higher numbers of girls than boys both attempt and pass examinations in arts subjects whereas in science subjects more boys than girls enter and are successful in examinations. In biology, however, it is interesting that there is a higher female entry, but a higher pass rate by boys.

At 'A' level, the extent of polarization between boys specializing in scientific and mathematical subjects, and girls specializing in the arts is even more marked than at 'O' level.

The numbers of subjects passed and the qualifications acquired are, however, only one factor relevant to job or post-school education entry. The kinds of subjects taken are also crucial. A job requiring five 'O' levels will usually specify particular subjects – English, maths and a science, for example.

TABLE 3.3 *Male and female entries and pass rates, GCE 'O' levels (all boards), June 1976*

Subject	Sex	Entry	%
Eng. lit.	F	141,000	64
	M	106,000	54
Eng. lang.	F	203,000	65
	M	183,000	56
French	F	84,000	64
	M	66,000	58
Religious studies	F	40,000	63
	M	25,000	51
Chemistry	F	30,000	60
	M	60,000	61
Physics	F	25,000	58
	M	86,000	59
Maths	F	87,000	56
	M	116,000	60
Biology	F	86,000	56
	M	61,000	61

Source: A. Clwyd, 'Reversing the Pecking Order', *Guardian*, p. 27, 7 July 1977. From unpublished paper, 'Sex Differences in Exam Performance' given by Roger Murphy, BPS Conference, 'Sex Role Stereotyping', Cardiff, July 1977.

TABLE 3.4 *GCE 'A' level subject specialization, all school leavers 1973-4 (passes in thousands)*

Subject combinations	1 'A' level		2 'A' level		3 'A' level	
	Boys	Girls	Boys	Girls	Boys	Girls
Science, with maths	1.07	0.30	2.24	0.46	11.19	3.01
Science, no maths	2.90	1.22	2.73	1.06	3.90	1.88
Social science	3.24	2.76	1.67	0.69	0.43	0.02
Arts	3.52	7.38	2.81	7.02	3.72	8.04
Other combinations, including science	—	—	2.22	2.18	6.29	4.21
Social science/arts	—	—	2.71	3.21	6.60	4.67
All subjects	10.73	11.66	14.38	14.62	32.13	21.83

Source: DES Statistics of Education 1974, vol. 2, *School Leavers*, Table 6, p. 8.

Some subjects have more currency than others, especially in the current economic climate where there are fewer than usual openings for unskilled labour or semi-skilled workers, but still a demand for skilled labour. Very few skilled jobs in industry can be obtained without some kind of apprenticeship or training, and entry to these almost always requires maths and science qualifications. Arts subjects are of limited value for direct entry to jobs and usually lead to different routes in higher and further education, so that after leaving school girls are likely to follow very different paths to those taken by boys of comparable ability level and social class background. For example, in 1973–4, 3.9 per cent of all female school leavers entered teacher training courses, but only 0.9 per cent of all male school leavers did so. Many of the courses offered in polytechnics have a scientific or technological bias, whether they are conventional degrees, sandwich courses, or Higher National Diplomas (HND), and this is reflected in the higher percentage of boys taking up polytechnic places. In 1973–4 2.3 per cent of all male school leavers went on to a polytechnic, but only 1.4 per cent of all female school leavers did likewise. Recently more girls than boys have been continuing their post-school education by attendance at colleges of further education and technical colleges: 13.5 per cent of 1973–4 female school leavers as compared with 6.8 per cent of male school leavers.[22] But even here girls are more likely to be taking courses in secretarial or clerical skills, hairdressing and nursery nursing, rather than in bricklaying or motor mechanics. Some two-thirds of courses in further education require maths or physics passes which girls seldom possess.[23] Table 3.5 gives some indication of the separation of post-school destinations of girls and boys. Even within some of these choices, differentiation between males and females exists. Most girls who take degree courses, for example, read arts or social sciences, rather than sciences, mathematics or technological disciplines. Of those taking up employment, whereas boys are more likely to enter jobs offering apprenticeship or other training and some career prospects as well as reasonable pay, girls are often forced into low-status, non-manual jobs with poor pay and few career prospects because of their qualifications or absence of them, becoming shorthand typists, nursery nurses, hairdressers or riding instructors.

TABLE 3.5 *Destinations of school leavers 1973–4 (in thousands)*

Leavers entering	Boys	Girls
Degree courses	28.63	15.93
Teacher training	3.07	13.17
Art and design courses	1.28	1.54
HND/HNC courses	1.44	0.80
OND/ONC courses	2.22	1.37
Catering courses	1.46	2.50
Nursing courses	0.04	4.92
Secretarial courses	0.11	14.62
GCE 'A' level courses	5.02	4.76
GCE 'O' level courses	4.43	3.89
Other FE courses	11.97	12.90
Temporary employment before full-time course	3.14	2.56
Employment	248.07	221.17
Destinations unknown	39.24	31.63
Total no. of leavers	350.12	331.76

Source: DES Statistics of Education 1974, vol. 2, *School Leavers*, Table 1, p. 11.

Thus, girls are frequently caught in a vicious circle. Their initial socialization and subsequent adoption of home-based cultures predisposes them towards certain kinds of school subjects, particularly those which utilize the verbal skills which develop more quickly in girls than in boys at primary school. On entering secondary school, instead of trying to develop new skills in numeracy and spatial and mechanical ability, girls concentrate on those verbal skills already established. They may be encouraged to do this by teachers and parents precisely because they are good in some subjects and weak in others. If in addition sciences and maths are perceived by many girls to be 'masculine' subjects, and where preemptive patterns of curricula or blocking together of specialist options effectively prevent or make difficult girls' opportunities to take technical subjects, then girls are pushed more and more towards the arts subjects, or towards biology as a suitable 'feminine' science. Once these patterns of subject

70

choice are established, public examination entries and pass rates reflect them, and may serve to stop girls from ever going beyond the narrow occupational confines of arts disciplines, whether they enter a job immediately after leaving school or go on to further or higher education first. It is not the intention to argue here that girls – or boys – should not take subjects which they enjoy, and are good at. But whilst entry to jobs and higher or further education remains heavily dependent on having obtained passes in particular subjects at CSE or GCE 'O' and 'A' level, then teachers, pupils and parents should recognize the perils of a system of schooling which allows students to specialize in certain subjects, to the exclusion of others, at a relatively early age, and at a time when the full implication of a given choice may not be known or recognized.

Of course, it is certainly true that girls are not the only ones to enter dead-end jobs with low pay and no prospects, working-class boys with few or no academic qualifications are also likely to obtain similar jobs. But the crucial difference is that boys are culturally expected to work for most of their adult lives, and so may subsequently have some incentive to improve their educational or practical skills in order to obtain better jobs. Girls, on the other hand, are not expected to work outside the home for long periods of time, and for many schoolgirls and girls working in unsatisfying jobs, marriage and a family are likely to appear as a much more attractive alternative, particularly since the cultures of many schoolgirls emphasize romance, personal appearance and relationships and an idyllic concept of marriage, as we saw in the previous chapter. Thus, little thought may be given to the possibility of not marrying, of becoming divorced or to the prospects of working for perhaps twenty or thirty years after child-rearing, and still less to the idea of working whilst bringing up children. Yet for many women these are both realistic and likely outcomes of their adult lives, and in 1977 women made up 41 per cent of the labour force. Projections on the future size of the labour force suggest that the proportion of married women working will have risen by 22.9 per cent by 1981 and by 32.9 per cent in 1986, compared with a growth rate of only 4.2 per cent for men over the same time period.[24] It is time that the education of all girls took notice of the length of their likely involvement in the labour force.

The present economic climate and state of economic recession in Britain mean that many school leavers of both sexes are going to experience great difficulty in finding a job of any kind. Half of unemployed school leavers are female, yet moves made by the government to combat unemployment amongst this sector of the population have not always taken account of this. The Job Creation Scheme, which provides funds to private and public employment sectors to enable the temporary employment of young people, has provided more work for boys than girls. Three-quarters of the sixteen- to eighteen-year-olds employed under the scheme are boys. Similarly, those benefiting from government-sponsored incentive grants to industry to encourage the taking on and training of young people, are almost entirely male. The two organizations set up to help the unemployed, the Manpower Services Commission, and the Training Services Agency, have been heavily criticized by the Equal Opportunities Commission for continuing to prepare women only for jobs which are traditionally 'women's work', and which are currently in short supply, rather than encouraging women to train for skilled manual jobs, for which a higher demand exists in the labour market.[25]

Furthermore, there is a danger that the existence of strongly-held and expressed moral social beliefs about unemployment and 'being on the dole' may force school leavers into taking any job that is available to them, however unsuitable, and in the case of girls this is likely to mean the traditional poorly-paid female jobs, like shop work, laundrywork, hairdressing, looking after animals or caring for young children. Even girls with high ability and good academic qualifications are likely to be affected in their choice of future careers by the economic recession, unless they have, exceptionally, acquired their qualifications in mathematics or the sciences. The cuts in public expenditure at local and national level and, ironically, a falling birth rate (which in other circumstances might have increased the opportunities available to women), have helped to bring about a massive closure of teacher-training establishments and drastic cut-backs in the numbers of teachers employed by local education authorities.

Teacher training has long been the most popular form of higher education for girls, and teaching itself one of the most likely professions for an educated girl to enter, but now many who would formerly have entered teaching will have to look elsewhere. Arts qualifications which would have been quite suitable for teaching may be less suitable for entry to other professions and, in applications to other sectors of higher education, many force girls to compete against each other for static or reducing numbers of places on arts and social sciences courses, whilst students with science or technical qualifications find a much less competitive situation when looking for a place in higher education.

Hence, it may be concluded that although there have been considerable changes in primary and secondary education since 1944, these have not yet brought about the eradication of discrimination and differentiation in the education of girls, as compared with the education of boys. Girls continue to be subjected to a curriculum which emphasizes to them their non-productive and sex-linked roles in the social relationships of production, even though this process is sometimes less apparent in the education of middle-class girls, of whom some kind of non-domestic career is now increasingly expected.

Because few significant changes have occurred in education in relation to girls, this does not mean that there have been no developments relevant to the struggle of women to obtain an education in which they are not subjected to discrimination and a different pattern of curricular choice on grounds of sex. Three developments seem to have particular significance for the education of girls: the debate over single-sex *versus* mixed schools; the 1977 'Great Debate' on education; the 1975 Sex Discrimination Act together with the accompanying establishment of the Equal Opportunities Commission.

Single-sex versus Mixed Schools: are Mixed Best?

Many educationalists regard this issue as already having been decided in favour of mixed schools.[26] However, the controversy has recently been reopened by the findings of the DES Survey (1975, p. 12) on curricular differences, which found that:

> Girls are more likely to choose a science, and boys a language, in a single sex school than they are in a mixed school, though in a mixed school a higher percentage of pupils may be offered these subjects.

Almost all primary schools are now co-educational, but about one-third of state secondary schools, and most independent schools, are still single-sex. There are some problems in comparing the extent to which the two types provide girls with equal educational opportunities because of evidence that single-sex schools sometimes have a higher social class and ability-mix than mixed schools.[27] However, this does not mean that comparison is impossible, simply that findings must be treated with some caution.

The most extensive study of mixed and single-sex schools is that work done by Dale, and he concludes that mixed schools are more successful than single-sex schools in every way – academically, attitudinally and socially.[28] It must be remembered that Dale's work was based only on grammar schools, and although he looked at both pupils and ex-pupils who had attended one or both types of school, his ex-pupils were all trainee teachers – perhaps not the most representative group that could have been studied. Dale noted that in mixed schools the presence of girls made boys more amenable in their behaviour and that the harsh discipline, obsession with academic work and high degree of concern with trivialities often complained of by pupils in single-sex schools were lessened in schools with pupils and teachers of both sexes.[29] He observed from his researches that pupils in mixed schools appeared to be less anxious about school than pupils in single-sex schools and also found that bullying, clique-formation and quarrelling amongst pupils were less marked in mixed schools. On the question of attainment, Dale's evidence suggests that both boys and girls do as well or better in mixed as in single-sex schools, because in the former boys and girls compete against each other and hence work harder.[30] Further, Dale (1974, p. 36) argues that 'the different approach made to problems by *the male and female mind*, both in staff and pupils, might contribute to a broader understanding' (my italics). Dale's conclusions on the supremacy of mixed schools are also shared by other researchers,[31] although in another study Dale and Miller found no association between class of degrees awarded and attendance at a mixed or single-sex school.[32]

However, not only the DES Survey on curricular differences contradicts Dale's findings. A study by King during the 1960s found that in mathematics (1965, p. 160):

> boys and girls from single-sex modern schools did consistently better than those from co-educational schools.

And Shaw has argued that (1976, p. 137):

> the social structures of mixed schools may drive children to make even more sex-stereotyped subject choices, precisely because of the constant pressure of the other sex and the pressure to maintain boundaries, distinctiveness and identity.

Certainly, Dale's own evidence on the experiences and attainments of girls does not entirely justify his conclusions that mixed schools are better, since one reason frequently given by pupils in their explanation of why they preferred mixed schools was that in single-sex schools there was too strong an emphasis on academic work and academic success.[33] What Dale seems to miss is the point that what pupils and ex-pupils like or dislike is not necessarily the same as what is educationally good or bad for them and that their preferences may express the sex-stereotyping to which they have been exposed. Although girls in single-sex schools may have less choice of subjects, they are likely to be much freer to choose which ones they take than in a mixed school where they may be competing with boys for resources and also perhaps subtly encouraged to fulfil their traditional sex-roles. In addition, the emphasis on academic learning in a single-sex school is not likely to convey to girls the impression that it is unimportant whether girls do well at school or not, a message which may well already be conveyed to girls by their socialization and culture, and not always contradicted in mixed schools. Furthermore, girls in single-sex schools are more likely than girls in mixed schools to be taught maths and science by women and are hence less likely to think of these subjects as 'masculine'.

Whilst it would probably not be desirable, just on grounds

75

of narrowness of curriculum choice if for no other reason, to return to a situation where all or most secondary schools are single-sex, we ought to give some thought to whether the 'normal social adjustment', which mixed schools are argued to give to pupils, does in fact encompass the worst aspects of sex stereotyping, as examined in the previous chapter. Evidence from American research in schools does suggest that this is the case:[34]

> In a mixed-sex environment . . . there appears to be a stronger need to differentiate between the sexes. Girls find it more difficult to compete for academic success with boys than with other girls because they fear, perhaps unconsciously, that this may be threatening to the boys, who will consequently reject them as potential sexual partners.

This is certainly an issue which is worthy of far more research attention than it has received so far, if only because it would help teachers and policy-makers to see how they could increase the educational opportunities available to girls in mixed schools and how they could start to reduce the amount of sex-stereotyping which goes on in many of those schools.

The 'Great Debate' on Education

Most of the concern shown by those interested in equality of opportunity in education after 1944 focused for a long time on the structure of education, principally resources and types of schools, and mechanisms of selection for secondary education.[35] However, much more recently the apparent failure of comprehensive schools to achieve working-class equality, the difficulties experienced by employers in recruiting skilled labour and school leavers of high ability into industry, right-wing critiques of state schooling and 'progressive' teaching methods,[36] and the increased militancy of school teachers[37] have all caused a shift in emphasis of educational debate from the structure of education to its content and transmission. In a speech at Ruskin College, Oxford in October 1976, the British Prime Minister, James Callaghan, expressed his concern about standards of education, methods of teaching in schools and the absence of strong links between education and industry, and spoke of his commitment to a core curriculum for all schools.[38] Early in 1977 the Secretary of State for Education, Shirley Williams, told the Schools Council (responsible since 1964 for many of the curricular innovations in education), that it would have to reduce its number of teachers' representatives and increase the number of lay members as well as taking more notice of the DES's views on curriculum.[39] The 'Great Debate' on education initiated by the Labour Government during 1977 to discuss the 'crisis' in education, centred on four main areas of education:

1 The curriculum;
2 The assessment of standards;
3 The education and training of teachers;
4 School and working life.

Public debates took place on these subjects in a variety of regions in England and Wales between invited audiences of educationalists, parents, politicians and industrialists. The extent to which education was fulfilling the requirements of equal educational opportunity for girls was rarely raised either in the discussions preceding the public debates or in the debates themselves. The document which was issued by the DES outlining the form the public debates would take, stated in relation to curriculum (DES, *Educating Our Children*, 1976, p. 2):

> In addition to establishing the basic skills, the curriculum
> should enable children . . . to understand the society of
> which they are part, including the economics of everyday
> life and the role of industry and commerce in sustaining
> our standard of living.

It is quite clear from our earlier examination in this chapter of the curriculum choices available to girls that in no sense is this currently being achieved for most girls attending schools in the state sector, yet this point failed to attract much attention. Although *Educating Our Children* did suggest that girls needed to be given more positive encouragement to enter new careers and jobs by employers and trade unionists, it would have been more or as useful to point out that greater positive encouragement from schools might also be in order.[40]

The idea of a core curriculum, that is a specification of what subjects should be taught in schools, and of which skills pupils should acquire during their school careers, was something much discussed during the regional meetings of the 'Great Debate', and in the policy deliberations which preceded and followed the regional meetings. Certainly, some kind of core curriculum which incorporated the teaching of mathematical and scientific skills to all school children, as well as literary and aesthetic skills, would have been very helpful to the many girls who at present are leaving school with qualifications in very narrow areas of learning. Although the Green Paper on Education published in July 1977 (a document which attempts to summarize the findings and conclusions of the regional meetings held earlier in that year), recognized the advantages of establishing a core curriculum, it rejected the imposition of such a curriculum on teachers, and failed to say what might be included in a core curriculum, other than specifying that English, maths and science should be included in all school time-tables.[41] Furthermore, if the Green Paper proposal to recruit more teachers experienced in other employment is adopted, as well as the recommendation that the Certificate of Education be phased out as a course for training teachers, then girls who want to enter teaching are going to be even more disadvantaged. Many of them will be unable to obtain the necessary experience in another job first and will not obtain the necessary academic qualifications to enter Bachelor of Education training courses, which the Green Paper suggests should include two 'A' levels and a maths 'O' level.

Thus, it may be concluded that although the Great Debate' on education has briefly discussed some issues of relevance to the education of girls, its emphasis on the links between industry and education may well result in changes which will not be beneficial to girls. If it had discussed to a greater extent why girls failed to take science, why they were often poor at maths and why women were rarely found in skilled jobs in industry, the Debate could have achieved much more.

The Sex Discrimination Act and the Equal Opportunities Commission

The Sex Discrimination Act of 1975 sought to make

sex discrimination unlawful in employment, training and related matters . . . *in education*, in the provision of goods, facilities and services, and in the disposal and management of premises [my italics].

The Act also set up an Equal Opportunities Commission to help enforce the legislation and to help bring about general equality of opportunity between the sexes. However, although the Act seemed to promise to achieve much towards equal opportunities for women, there are a number of problems both with the Act itself and with the procedures by which a complaint may be made.

In relation to education, for example, the Act allows that where students of either sex are admitted to an establishment they must have equal opportunity with other students to enjoy the facilities available for other students. But if one single-sex girls' school, for instance, does not have facilities for chemistry lessons, then in order to make a complaint under the Act, it would be necessary to show that all *comparable* schools within the same authority had those facilities. There is, therefore, no compulsion under the Act for Local Authorities to provide additional resources which would make the achievement of equal educational opportunity a possibility regardless of sex. Nor does the Act allow for positive discrimination to be used in education in favour of a disadvantaged sex.

The procedure for making a complaint under the Act in relation to education differs from the procedure for dealing with other areas of the legislation. Any complaint about education in the public sector must go first to the appropriate Secretary of State, and subsequently goes not to a tribunal (as do employment cases under the Sex Discrimination Act), but to a county court. As Coussins notes, this in itself is a deterrent.[42]

However, there is also another problem which relates to the *nature* of discrimination in education as opposed to in employment or elsewhere; Coussins (1976, p. 85) points out that:

'cases' do not occur in a more long-term and ongoing way. Individuals may not stand out as being particularly affected; it is more likely to be children in a whole area, children of a certain age, mature women students, the readers of a particular textbook or some other group. Neither is the remedy likely to be a simple short-term action.

Not only have few genuine grievances under the Act been taken to the Equal Opportunities Commission but the Commission itself has not initiated very much research or investigation into discrimination in education. It has looked into the allocation of grammar school places in Tameside (where twice as many of these have been awarded to girls as to boys), and has begun to examine possible discriminatory practices in secondary schools. Further, it has asked the DES to review the system of student grants, which presently discriminates against many women in the further education sector who are taking non-degree level courses for which grants are discretionary rather than mandatory. But the Commission has left many areas of discrimination in schools untouched; for example, it has decided not to try to use legislation to influence schools' choices of reading schemes for young children, even though some of these are known to be sexist.[43]

But it is not just that the procedure for making complaints about discrimination is cumbersome and bureaucratic, or that the EOC has failed to initiate sufficient investigation into discrimination in schools — although both the legislation and the Commission have been criticized heavily on these points.[44] It is also the formulation and scope of the legislation which is at fault:[45]

the 'basis of the Act is that it is unlawful to treat one sex less favourably than another' but that it is 'not prima facie . . . discriminatory to treat boys and girls differently.' In other words differentiation between the sexes is not equated with discrimination, and is therefore not illegal.

Furthermore, individual cases taken to court, even if successful, are unlikely to prevent similar practices going on in other areas of education or in other Local Authorities. And positive discrimination in favour of one sex is not allowable in education under the Act as it is in training and employment, yet as Coussins (1976, p. 90) says:

Positive discrimination in some form in the education system is absolutely necessary if girls and women are to regain the ground they have lost, or have never had, over the years. . . .

We can then, expect little in the form of radical changes in sexism and discriminatory or differentiating practices of schools to emerge from the Sex Discrimination Act or the Equal Opportunities Commission.

The Education of Girls: Where are We Now?

In this chapter it has been suggested that although the education of girls has advanced enormously in England and Wales since the nineteenth century, there are still discriminatory and differentiating practices which are restricting the educational achievements of women. Middle-class girls of high or average ability are now likely to encounter fewer difficulties than was formerly the case, since teachers, policy-makers and the community in general increasingly recognize that they will work for a large part of their lives and are likely to combine marriage and motherhood with a career. But few working-class girls are likely to enter 'careers' as opposed to 'dead-end' jobs, and there remain strong beliefs that for them work outside the home is of little importance, and that their main interests lie in marriage, child-rearing and finding out how to perform domestic tasks more easily. And for both classes of girls, of whatever ability level, their socialization combines with their culture and schooling to push them into specializing in arts subjects during the later years of secondary school. Arts subjects are insufficient preparation or qualification for a wide variety of occupations and post-school training, and in particular for those jobs or further/higher education which will provide satisfying, well-paid work later.

Discrimination against girls may take subtle forms, as the previous chapter showed in its examination of sexism and sex-stereotyping, and is often difficult to detect and unamenable to investigation or complaint under the Sex Distrimination Act. Differentiation between boys and girls, as this chapter has shown, is easier to detect but just as difficult to eradicate, and curricular differences between the sexes remain a serious problem. Although mixed schools provide a wider curriculum choice than single-sex schools, single-sex schools are often more successful at encouraging girls to take traditionally 'masculine' subjects, and the 'social adjustment' which mixed schools are argued to achieve may be merely a further confirmation of sex-role differences. The 'Great Debate' on education has failed to look in any depth at the reasons why schools are not sending out many girls into industry – other than as unskilled temporary workers – and has neglected to consider the beneficial effects which a core curriculum including sciences, maths and technical subjects might have on the education of many schoolgirls. The Sex Discrimination Act has not provided the promised panacea for the ills of women's education. Girls may have gained equal access with boys to primary and secondary schooling, and do enter further education in larger numbers than boys. But what they have gained access *to* is not always the same in educational content and occupational currency as that to which boys have access. And until curricular and non-curricular discrimination and differentiation on grounds of sex are ended, both girls and boys will continue to receive an education which is incomplete, inflexible, and inhibiting to the full development of their potential as human beings.

Chapter 4

Women in Higher Education

If women in nineteenth-century Britain did not easily achieve access to formal schooling, their battle to enter higher education required greater persistence still, and lasted long after the 1944 Education Act had, in theory, offered all children, male and female, equal access to primary and secondary education. The British university system was founded on principles of elitism, and these have continued to be strongly upheld by a capitalist class society for which it is axiomatic that society consists of one dominant group and many subordinate groups.[1] The sexual division of labour which forms part of the social relations of production in British society demands that women be excluded from the ruling group as active participants. Because higher education has always been seen as one source of recruitment to and socialization of the dominant group in society, it has been exceedingly difficult for women to make claims regarding their right to a higher education.

Whilst the full entry of girls into primary and secondary education, irrespective of their social class background, was eventually accepted on the grounds that a 'suitable' education would play an important part both in teaching them the skills necessary to carry out their adult roles as housewives and mothers (and that it would also confirm to them the ideological appropriateness of their place in the sexual division of labour), no such ideological justifications were extended to higher education. Indeed, the inclusion of women amongst those admitted to higher education either as students only, or subsequently as teachers, represented in the nineteenth century and still represents, a threat to the elite character of that education and also a threat to the existing social relations of production and the ideology underlying them. If women received higher education they might have their expectations about their lives raised, and their perception of their role in the social relations of production altered, with disastrous consequences for the capitalist mode of production.[2]

Hence, although university education in Britain existed long before the nineteenth century, so great was the resistance to women entering universities that it was not until the passage of legislation in 1875 allowing universities to grant degrees to women, that any of these institutions began to admit women students on a comparable basis to men. Even after this date, some universities continued to see female students as a category quite separate from male students, so that Oxford did not admit women to degrees until 1920, and Cambridge not until 1948.[3] And although women students have become less scarce in universities and in polytechnics in the second half of the twentieth century,[4] higher education remains an area of learning from which many women are excluded, both as potential students and as potential teachers. As Blackstone and Fulton (1975, p. 270) say:

> Women are discouraged from a wide range of high-status subjects with relatively good job opportunities . . . are less encouraged to enter college or university, to undertake graduate work, and to enter the academic profession, and not only by informal and subtle means . . . forms of overt discrimination have been used, both in admissions and in the granting of financial aid.

Although at various times since the 1960s — and particularly since the passage of the Sex Discrimination Act in 1975 — the relative scarcity of women in higher education has given rise to concern in official policy-making circles,[5] encouragement to women to enter higher education has rarely been given a high priority. Indeed, policies and policy-decisions which have been made in the late 1970s appear to attach little or no importance to the higher education of women. The reduction in the numbers of initial teacher-training places available has removed one important source of post-school education for women, and few alternative courses requiring comparable entry qualifications have become available. The strong emphasis on the importance of having more higher education courses in the sciences, mathematics and engineering is unlikely to produce an increase in the numbers of women applying for entry to establishments of higher education.[6]

The Fight of Women to enter Higher Education

It is important to realize that in looking at the past and continuing difficulties experienced by women seeking access to higher education, we are considering not just sexual barriers but also class ones. Middle-class women have fought their way into the hallowed fields of higher education with great effort, but the struggle of working-class women to enter higher education has hardly begun.[7] It took middle-class women a long time to prove that they were worthy of higher educational facilities; in medical education for example, women offering themselves as candidates for medical diplomas at London University in the 1850s were refused those diplomas. Consequently by 1870 there were only two qualified female practitioners in Britain, neither of whom had obtained their qualifications in Britain. Despite many attempts by women to take higher educational courses in medicine, they were unable to do so until after the Bill of 1875 allowing universities to award women degrees. Women trying to acquire medical qualifications and the endeavours of girls' private secondary schools in opening university local examinations to their pupils, were influential in bringing about the 1875 Bill, but it seems likely that it was only the anticipated small size and class composition of female demand for higher education which brought about the partial capitulation of some universities.[8] Others continued long after 1875 to deny women degrees on the grounds that their founders had set them up only for boys, but as A. J. P. Taylor has pointed out, other stipulations of founders were already being ignored, for example marriage bans and religious tests.[9] Although by the end of the nineteenth century some women were receiving university degrees, the numbers of women to whom this chance was given were very small. During the nineteenth century the only girls who received a secondary education of a sufficiently high standard to allow them to proceed to higher education, were a tiny minority of middle-class girls whose wealthy and slightly enlightened parents sent them to schools like the North London Collegiate School which, unlike most nineteenth-century schools educating girls, did offer a curriculum which went beyond the narrow confines of basic literacy and ladylike accomplishments. The 1870 Education Act did little to improve the educational lot of working-class girls, and although the 1902 Education Act and the Free Place Regulations of 1907 saw a very slight improvement in the prospects of obtaining a secondary education for a few working-class children, it was not until well after the 1944 Education Act (offering free secondary education to all) that anyone began to consider under-representation of working-class or female students in higher education as a problem.

This is not to say, however, that universities offered the only form of post-school education available to women during the nineteenth and early twentieth centuries, since teacher-training establishments provided some limited opportunities for women too, and some of those women who benefited from these were working-class. By 1846 there were some nine training colleges in existence where women could train to become elementary school teachers, although as Borer points out, the level of education actually offered by such colleges was probably nearer to secondary schooling than to a university degree.[10] In addition, neither middle-class nor working-class women who entered teaching, often choosing it because they had not succeeded in achieving marriage (then considered a life-goal for women), were well paid. Teachers in the nineteenth century were exploited and had little status or autonomy.[11] After the 1870 Education Act many more elementary teachers were required and further establishments were opened to train suitable candidates. Limited though the educational horizons of most training colleges were, for a long time they provided the only chance of post-school education for working-class women, as well as the possibility of upward mobility through the class structure.[12] But their very existence was and has been used as an excuse for failing to provide sufficient degree-level education for women in universities or comparable institutions, on the grounds that women are well catered for already, and do not need or want degree courses other than those leading to a teaching qualification. The presence of teacher-training establishments, then, has hindered rather than helped the provision of higher education courses for women.[13] The lesser entry requirements of these establishments – in comparison to degree courses in universities and elsewhere – may also have subtly acted to lower the aspirations and efforts of girls still at school, so that good 'A' level performances have been seen by some girls with places at colleges of education as unnecessary.

Women and Changes in Higher Education Policy

The relative absence of girls in higher education has not, since the beginning of the 1960s, gone unnoticed and some efforts have been made since that time to attract more working-class students in general, and more women in particular, into higher education. The 1963 Robbins Report on higher education stressed the relationship between the universities and economic growth, and pointed out that the 'wastage' of girl school leavers who did not go on to higher education – despite having the academic ability to do so – was not in the best interests of the nation's future economic prosperity.[14] At the time of the Report, Britain was still enjoying reasonable economic growth, and graduates were finding it relatively easy to acquire jobs commensurate with their level of education. This expansionist attitude contrasts starkly with the concern of educational policy-makers in the late 1970s to reduce or keep static the number of young people entering higher education, and to tailor the courses offered closely to the demands of the labour market.

But between the Robbins Report and the cut-backs in expenditure in the higher education sector of the late 1970s, many changes have taken place in the provision and structure of higher education, some of which have affected the opportunities available to women students. As well as expansion in the numbers of universities and the range of courses offered,

87

the 'binary' system of higher education has been set up, establishing numbers of non-university institutions, notably the polytechnics. The Council for National Academic Awards has taken on the task of validating degree courses in these institutions, which have been placed under the control of Local Education Authorities rather than enjoying the relative autonomy of the universities. Universities have continued to see themselves as centres of academic excellence, concerned with elite socialization, the transmission of high-status knowledge and research. The former Colleges of Advanced Technology which became universities in the mid-1960s (on the recommendation of the Robbins Report) have broken away from the traditional pattern by concentrating on applied rather than pure knowledge; however, because of their technological bias, they have attracted fewer women students than their more conventional counterparts.[15] The new universities, although they have scarcely succeeded in attracting more working-class students into higher education, have been more successful than the former CATs in attracting female students, because they were to the forefront of the 1960s expansion in arts and social sciences courses — areas of study which have attracted large numbers of women. Polytechnics, on the other hand, were established as a gesture of benevolence towards the working class even if their public image has suffered because they have been seen as 'second-class' universities. But Donaldson, in an analysis of polytechnic development since the 1960s, questions the extent to which most polytechnics have achieved the objectives set out for them. For example, amongst those objectives were working-class higher-educational opportunities on a full and part-time basis; strong links between courses and local industry or commerce; a higher degree of community control and involvement than most universities.[16] Certainly, if women are counted as part of the working class and a community to whom more opportunities are to be extended, then the polytechnics have not been overwhelmingly successful. In 1974 2.3 per cent of all male school leavers went on to a full-time polytechnic course, but only 1.4 per cent of female school leavers did so.[17] For an analysis of male and female student numbers in non-university higher education see Table 4.1.

The Sex Discrimination Act of 1975 has removed some of

TABLE 4.1 *Student numbers in non-university higher education, 1968, 1971 and 1974 (in thousands)*

Course	1968		1971		1974	
	Men	Women	Men	Women	Men	Women
CNAA 1st Degree	2.79	0.68	6.05	2.25	18.92	11.76
HND	4.60	1.08	5.97	1.85	4.71	1.63
NDD/Dip.AD	3.41	3.21	3.76	3.35	–	–
Art. T. Dip./Cert.	0.23	0.26	0.32	0.30	0.25	0.23
Other advanced	13.70	6.84	15.39	8.33	15.77	10.00
Total	24.73	12.07	31.49	16.08	39.65	23.62

Source: DES Statistics of Education 1974, vol. 3, *Further Education*, p. 12.

the most overt forms of discrimination used against potential women students, for example the quotas used by medical schools to restrict the numbers of female applicants allowed to take up places.[18] But as Blackstone and Fulton suggest, not all the barriers preventing women from entering higher education necessarily involve overt forms of discrimination.[19] The processes of sex-stereotyping and curricular differentiation in school are likely to have a strong influence on the aspirations of girls in relation to higher education, so that girls are either encouraged not to be high achievers — except in 'feminine' subjects like home economics — or else they are channelled into arts subject choices rather than into sciences and maths. Thus, some girls never even contemplate higher education; others are persuaded that they are best suited to a very vocationally specific course in teaching training, and only the highly motivated usually remain to try for university and polytechnic places. Of these, since it is apparent that many girls who do take 'A' levels specialize in arts subjects, most will be competing against each other and highly qualified male applicants, to enter arts and social sciences degree courses, whilst the few who have taken sciences at 'A' level may find a university or polytechnic place much more easily. The expansion in arts and social sciences degree courses during the 1960s certainly helped many women to enter higher education who might not otherwise have done so. But

89

the tide has now swung away from these areas and in so far as expansion is possible, or contradiction to be prevented, it is in the areas of sciences and technology that new developments are taking place, areas that few women are able to enter at university or polytechnic because they lack the appropriate 'A' level qualifications.

One institution which has, since 1971, been able both to encourage women students and to offer science, technology and maths courses to those without existing formal qualifications in these areas, has been the Open University, although its recruitment has been primarily amongst more mature students rather than school leavers. Indeed, it was at one time feared that[20] 'as the Open University started its courses in 1971 . . . it would become "a haven for housebound *Guardian* housewives"'. But as it happened, only 27 per cent of the first year's intake were women, and very few of them housewives, so that in fact the percentage of women students at the Open University in that first year was slightly less than that found in conventional universities. The percentage of women on Open University courses has not gone up significantly since 1971, and although this is partly a reflection of the regional quota system, it is also a product of the many difficulties faced by women wanting to return to a course of study: lack of finance; low levels of confidence; problems of minding children and organizing domestic work; absence of transport for getting to study centres. McIntosh's evidence, however, certainly indicates that women who do take open university courses persist in their studies at a higher rate than men, and obtain credits in foundation courses more quickly than male students, even in traditionally 'masculine' areas like science, technology and maths.[21]

The Lucky Few: Women in Higher Education

Some women do, of course, get into higher education, both as students and more exceptionally as teachers, and the numbers are growing slowly. Between 1968 and 1976 the percentage of women amongst UK applicants to university increased from 30 per cent to 36.2 per cent and the percentage of women amongst those UK applicants who were successful in obtaining places over the same period rose from 29.7 per cent to 36.9 per cent.[22] The University Central Council on Admissions also reported in 1976 that when applications with no chance of success (because of poor 'A' level grades) were discounted, women university applicants actually had an advantage over men in obtaining places in medicine, languages, engineering and technology.[23] In polytechnics and in other institutions offering advanced courses too, numbers have increased.

But even those women who do get into higher education display, on the whole, patterns of subject choice which are different from those of most men in higher education. The pattern of curricular differentiation established between the sexes in schools is thus carried on. Women in polytechnics and universities are most likely to be found on courses in arts, social sciences, education, business studies, catering or design. Sciences, maths and technology courses all have a heavy preponderance of male students. Women rarely take sandwich courses, which combine academic studies with work experience; in 1974 23,524 men took these, but only 3,621 women. In certain subjects, for instance in languages and in some of the social sciences, women do comprise a major part of the student body.[24] But in postgraduate study (except for courses of teacher training) even in subjects where women make up a large percentage of the undergraduate population, they are conspicuous by their absence.[25]

And if women are few in number amongst postgraduate students, amongst academic staff of institutions of higher education they are even more rare. Indeed, it is at this point that the process of filtering out women from the world of

TABLE 4.2. *Graduate teachers in public sector higher and further education, 1974*

	Under 60	Over 60
Male graduates	18,234	646
Female graduates	3,436	80

Source: DES Statistics of Education 1974, vol. 3, *Further Education*, p. 12.

higher education reaches its peak of efficiency. In universities, for example, only 10 per cent of ordinary lecturers are women, less than 6 per cent of readers and senior lecturers and under 2 per cent of professors. In polytechnics the position of women is very similar, although the absence of separately-published statistics for further and higher education in the public sector means that the figures give a less accurate picture. Not only are there fewer women teaching in higher education but in view of the numbers of women students taking first degrees in arts and social sciences, this suggests processes of discrimination and filtering out. There is also evidence that women who overcome these processes face further discrimination and differentiation in the form of lower salaries and fewer chances of promotion than their male colleagues (see Table 4.3).[26]

TABLE 4.3 *Average salaries of full-time FE/HE teachers in public sector, 1974*

£s	Under 25	25–29	30–34	35–39	40–44	45–49	50–54	55–59	60 and over
Male graduates	2,128	2,475	2,945	3,322	3,528	3,706	3,801	3,829	3,845
Female graduates	2,094	2,377	2,706	2,888	2,982	3,006	3,180	3,235	2,686

Source: DES Statistics of Education 1974, vol. 3, *Further Education*, p. 12.

Although Blackstone and Fulton's evidence is now somewhat dated, more recent sources suggest that the trends they observed are still continuing (see Table 4.4). A report published in 1977 suggested that the salaries and promotion chances of women lecturers at the London University Institute of Education were below those of their male colleagues, despite the existence of the Sex Discrimination Act.[27] And another controversy in the same year, about the procedures for making appointments at the University of Cardiff, also gives rise to the suspicion that women may be disadvantaged where and if posts are allocated on the basis of an 'old-boy' network amongst male academics.[28] The pattern of employment between the sexes in universities is not confined to a

TABLE 4.4 *Average UK university teachers' salaries by age, sex, publication, 1969*

	High			Publications Medium			Low		
Age	Men	Women	Deficit	Men	Women	Deficit	Men	Women	Deficit
Under 30	1,800	–	–	1,800	1,700	6%	1,600	1,400	12%
30–39	2,700	2,400	11%	2,600	2,300	12%	2,300	2,100	9%
40–49	3,900	3,100	21%	3,600	2,700	25%	3,000	2,400	20%
50/over	4,300	3,300	23%	3,800	3,100	18%	3,400	3,200	6%

Source: Blackstone, T. and Fulton, O., 'Sex discrimination among university teachers', *British Journal of Sociology*, vol. 26, no. 3, September 1975, p. 268.

few institutions but is common to them all. A female lecturer at a university in South West England said in 1976 of her institution:[29]

I find there are no women professors at all. . . . At a rough estimate there are eight women readers or senior lecturers . . . out of 195; 48 women lecturers . . . out of 502; and three women research fellows out of 18.

In polytechnics too, the absence of women lecturers is also a clearly established trend. There are very few women heads of department, and no woman has yet been appointed a director of a polytechnic.[30] In both universities and polytechnics there is also evidence to indicate that it is women rather than men who are to be found in untenured, part-time, temporary and marginal posts.[31]

Becoming and being a Female Student

Now that the Sex Discrimination Act has made illegal overt forms of discrimination on grounds of sex in the admission of students to courses in higher education, the percentage of women amongst the student body is slowly increasing.[32] However, in some institutions where the main bias of courses is towards the applied sciences and technology, such as in the technological universities and the polytechnics, the percentage of women remains low. The main barriers to the access of women into higher education now appear to relate to three main factors. First, the tendency of women to specialize in school subjects which do not give them a free or wide choice of courses in higher education, and which ensure that women compete against large numbers of other students for their higher education places. Second, girls may consciously be encouraged by parents, teachers and friends to lower their aspirations in relation to post-school education — irrespective of their actual or potential ability — on the grounds that their future roles as wives and mothers will not be compatible with the kinds of occupations that they might enter after completing a degree or degree-type course.[33] Courses such as teacher-training or secretarial-training may be argued to be more suitable for girls since they offer conditions of work (and the possibility of part-time employment) which will be compatible with marriage and a family. Hence the socialization of girls into the sexual division of labour in society, even though this may be modified for middle-class girls and those of high academic ability, is successful in diverting the attention of many girls away from most courses in higher education. Third, and this observation is only speculative (though deserving of further investigation), the home-based culture of many girls in addition to their strong internalization of the sexual division of labour, may make them more reluctant than boys to leave home in order to read for a degree or a similar qualification.

Although, clearly, women who actually become students will have successfully overcome these barriers, this does not mean that they will have been totally unaffected by their existence. Indeed, women students are likely also to be affected by the same factors which have prevented others of their sisters from becoming students in the first place. Their choice of 'A' level subjects and their choice of arts or social sciences courses in higher education is likely to place them in close proximity with most of the other women students to be found in higher education. This may have an impact on those girls who do make untraditional choices of courses, because their departure from the 'norm' will be clearly visible, and they may be seen as deviant or 'odd' by those women who have made more conventionally 'female' choices.

Although women who become students will have triumphed over the notion that higher education is not suited to women, they may nevertheless be sufficiently socialized into the ideology of the sexual division of labour to believe that their educational progress and achievements are of less importance than is the case for male students. Higher educational establishments are usually mixed-sex institutions and, as in co-educational schools, the presence of men may tend to make women act and think in sex-stereotyped ways to a greater extent than would be the case in a single-sex establishment. Hence, some women students may subordinate their own academic achievements to those of men, making remarks such as:[34]

'My degree doesn't really matter very much; I'll probably get married after graduation'
or 'I would like to get an upper second, but it would upset my boyfriend if I got a better degree than he has.'

These sentiments may be intensified by the attitudes of some higher education lecturers towards female students if they express views like this:[35]

We expect women who come here [to university] to be competent, good students, but we don't expect them to be brilliant or original.

Finally, women students may, especially those who have been socialized into a home-based domestically oriented culture (even if their attachment to this culture is not so strong as to prevent them entering higher education at all) tend to retreat into that culture when at university or polytechnic to an extent which goes beyond making a separation between their own academic achievements and those of male students. Whilst male students participate in many of the sporting and cultural activities which higher education establishments offer, some female students, although certainly not all, may prefer to stay in their lodgings, hall of residence or flat, working, cooking or engaging in other traditionally 'female', home-based leisure pursuits such as dressmaking or knitting. This may be relatively unimportant, but to the extent that women students choose traditionally female activities, they may be cutting themselves off from more than team games, rock-climbing or drinking in the Student Union bar, and may be failing to take advantage of a valuable part of their higher education.

Roger Smith's research on women journalists and their failure to be successful on Fleet Street puts forward the suggestion that this failure may be partially due to the exclusion of female journalists from certain informal learning situations which are freely available to male journalists.[36] These learning situations offer the possibility of acquisition of skills, information and political acumen which cannot be learnt by formal instruction. Smith argues that such kinds of knowledge are acquired by male journalists at times when women journalists are not likely to be around – on night shifts for instance, or in places where women are unwelcome, such as in drinking clubs or public houses. A similar analysis may be applied to higher education where discussion of ideas and facts by students outside lectures, seminars and practical or laboratory work may be as important as more structured discussion and learning. Much of this informal discussion takes place in bars, in pool-rooms, after a game of football, or simply over coffee. Women will be subtly or not so subtly excluded from some of these situations, and will sometimes simply not be there, if their cultural alternative to lectures and other organized work is to return to their lodgings, flat or hall of residence. That women do rarely take part in informal discussion of their work is suggested by evidence that they are often reluctant to participate in intellectual argument even in formal settings.[37] Webb argues that the particular 'cognitive style' used by women students may militate against them in their subsequent academic performance, particularly in disciplines where persistent and determined defence of and argument about abstract ideas is a criterion of high academic achievement.[38] It seems feasible to argue that one source of the distinctive 'cognitive style' of many women students may simply be their cultural exclusion from situations in which an alternative style might be learnt or practised. Furthermore, as Frazer and Sadker note, other qualities associated with successful academic performance such as aggression, confidence, self-assertiveness, competitiveness and ambition, are encouraged in male school pupils, but not in female pupils.[39]

96

In other aspects of student life, however, women students seem to fare better. For example, women have not been prevented from taking up student union offices at either local or national level, and have thus participated actively in student politics. Student groups have not been unwilling to take up issues of interest to women students — low grants for married women students, nursery and crèche provision, contraception, abortion — although in most cases the issues have also been of interest to men students too. But student organizations have shown a surprising lack of concern about the general problem of why women are under-represented in higher education and what can be done about it, and about sexist teaching and curricula. And these omissions may be due as much to the failure of women students to draw attention to such issues as to chauvinism on the part of men students.

Sexism and its Challenges in the Curriculum of Higher Education

Just as many schools offer and teach subjects which are sexist in their content or in their underlying assumptions, so higher education continues this trend. How many universities or polytechnics study women writers or poets, examine the history of working-class women rather than working-class men, or are concerned with 'economic woman' as well as 'economic man'? Where the interests, concerns and achievements of women are taken into account, it is often in the context of a specialized Women's Studies course, mainly taken and taught by women, rather than as part of ordinary, core courses taken by all students.[40]

The importance of sexism in areas of knowledge in higher education can only be understood fully in relation to the ways in which educational institutions are organized. As Bernstein has argued,[41] traditional educational systems are characterized by strong authority, value and subject boundaries, such that Bernstein (1971, p. 56) remarks:

> Knowledge transmitted within such systems is private property with its own power structure and market situation.

Moves to establish more open educational systems, he claims, can have drastic consequences for the institutions concerned (1971, p. 59):

> disturbance in classification of knowledge will lead to a disturbance of existing authority structures, existing specific educational identities and concepts of property.

The ideology of the social relations of production, including the sexual division of labour, is based heavily on the content of education as well as on its authority relationships and the values which it transmits. If the content is altered, then the ideology of the existing social relationship of production is threatened, as well as the identity and status of those who teach the traditional conceptions of knowledge.

It is precisely this kind of threat which is provided by demands to move to non-sexist forms of knowledge in higher education. Whether these demands take the form of specialized Women's Studies courses, or whether they affect courses taken by all students, they effectively challenge the legitimacy of the existing power structures in higher education to transmit sexist knowledge, by offering alternative definitions of reality. Second, challenges to the transmission of sexist knowledge question the validity of claims made by academics that knowledge transmitted in higher education is objective truth; their own admittance of subjectivity causes other claims to objectivity to be examined more closely.

Women's Studies courses themselves are usually interdisciplinary attempts to look at issues and themes of concern to women. They may, because of their interdisciplinary character, threaten the property claims and subject identities of those who have carved careers out of hiding behind subject boundaries. There is often no reluctance to allow Women's Studies courses to be taught, providing that they are optional and/or non-examinable; as such they are thought likely to attract only committed feminists and even provide male lecturers with an excuse for continuing to teach in a sexist way, because 'the women are already catered for'. Only if Women's Studies courses demand compulsory status are they seen as threatening, because then uncommitted students may begin to develop critical views of the rest of the curriculum in particular, and of academe in general. Women's Studies also dispute the definitions of education and of the social relations of production which capitalist societies offer:[42]

> On the one hand, by imparting technical and social skills and appropriate motivations, education increases the productive capacity of workers. On the other hand, education helps defuse and depoliticize the potentially explosive class relations of the productive process, and thus serves to perpetuate the social, political and economic conditions through which a portion of the product of labour is expropriated in the form of profits.

Sexism is strong not only in the arts and social sciences, where the main focus of attention is on male philosophies, creativity, theories and actions, but in the sciences too. With the exception of biology, botany and zoology which women tend to prefer to other sciences in higher education,[43] most science is taught in close relationship to its role in capitalist societies and has no relevance to those who reject capitalism or who are not allowed to participate in its economic production:[44]

> [Science] no longer corresponds to the Socratic desire for knowledge alone. It functions as an aspect of production (production of truth) itself serving the higher goal of production.

Science has a masculine image, right from its introduction into the secondary school up to the level of university or polytechnic. This image, presented by the ways in which it is taught, the manner in which scientific textbooks are illustrated, and its content, often does discourage girls from taking it seriously, as Sharpe's study of working-class schoolgirls demonstrates.[45]

The sexism of curricula in higher education is of importance not just within its own sphere of influence, but also because of its influence on other sectors of education. As Bernstein (1971, p. 69) says:

> The major control on the structuring of knowledge at the secondary level is the structuring of knowledge at the tertiary level, specifically the university. Only if there is a major change in the structuring of knowledge at this level can there be effective . . . change at lower levels.

A higher education system which continues to permit the transmission of sexist knowledge not only fails to contribute to the intellectual potential and development of its own students, but also helps to perpetuate the transmission of sexist knowledge in other sectors of education. Furthermore, the teaching of sexist knowledge reinforces the ideological reproduction of the social relations of production which is begun in the school.[46]

Women as Academics: a Token Elite

The most striking thing about women teachers and researchers in higher education is their numerical rarity. Even in subjects which at undergraduate level are dominated by female students, women seem to fail to act beyond the level of a first degree, and are conspicuous by their absence in the academic profession itself. As Webb says of sociology, a subject dominated by women at the undergraduate level (1977, p. 1):

> Although women represent something like two thirds of the Sociology undergraduate population, within the ranks of professional sociologists their appearance is a relative rarity . . . the major 'leakage' of women is between undergraduate and postgraduate study.

In effect then, two problems which affect the representation of women in the academic profession need to be considered at the outset. The first problem is that of why women are under-represented — even at the level of studying for a first degree or its equivalent — in the sciences, mathematics and technological subjects. The extent to which this rests on the previous socialization and culture of many girls, as well as on their subject choices at school and on other forms of curricular and hidden-curricular forms of differentiation between boys and girls, has already been discussed in some detail. The second problem is that of why women drop out of academic life after undergraduate study, since clearly this reduces the 'pool' of women from which potential academics are likely to emerge.

The limited evidence which is available on women as undergraduate students suggests, although it does no more than this, that women are often less committed to a high level of academic performance than are men.[47] It is also possible that women approach their studies differently from men, concentrating more on written work and examinations, rather than trying to excel in verbal discussion and argument.[48] This may affect the extent to which women are 'noticed' as potential graduate students, particularly in courses where the class of degree is heavily dependent on examinations taken at the end of the final year, so that 'clues' to potential research students may be sought not only on the basis of work already examined or assessed, but also on the ability of students to conduct arguments and defend points of view.[49] However, problems of commitment and variations in approach to learning seem to stem as much from the general socialization and schooling of women in industrial capitalist society (and from the societal allocation of women to subordinate, domestic and 'caring' roles in the sexual division of labour), as from the structuring and learning in higher education, particularly since similar characteristics of learning and commitment seem to be present in girls at school as well as amongst those in higher education.[50]

Indeed, the socialization of girls and the sexual division of labour dominant in industrial societies also provide a further source of explanation for the absence of women amongst postgraduate students and academics. Even for those women who have been determined enough to enter higher education, the end of a first degree course often marks a watershed in their lives. Pressure is likely to be put on them by families, friends, tutors, careers advisers and others, to leave higher education after obtaining their initial qualification, either because of impending marriage, the birth of children, or because 'over qualified' women are felt to be unemployable and worse still, unmarriageable.[51] Women who do decide to continue with their studies must either put off marriage and having children, or else try to cope with the difficult task of combining these with academic study at a time when they have no career mapped out which would justify their decision.[52] Furthermore, married women who want to do graduate work may be faced with having to carry this out in institutions which are unsympathetic to or unable to supervise adequately their research, because a husband's occupation determines at which institutions or place they are able to study. Even for women who are not married, graduate work still presents problems of motivation and of justifying deviation from the 'normal' practice of other female graduates. Furthermore, if as Webb suggests, women's interests in a particular discipline do not coincide with current definitions of high-status areas within that discipline, then they may experience difficulty in obtaining a place for graduate study, or their researches may fail to be taken seriously by peers and supervisors and other established academics.[53] The latter is likely to seriously affect their chances of obtaining an academic post on completion of their studies.

This, of course, raises another issue, that of the extent to which potential lecturers or researchers in higher education are able to leap the final barrier from postgraduate study to employment, an undertaking which is becoming ever more difficult as the number of vacancies for suitable posts contracts, and the number of candidates increases. Similar factors to those which prevent women continuing from undergraduate to graduate study may come into play again, with pressure from family, friends and others to leave the academic world and seek employment or marriage or engage in domestic labour and childrearing. But there is also another factor, which is probably less apparent in admission to graduate study since the Sex Discrimination Act of 1975, but still apparent in appointments to academic posts — direct discrimination against women.[54] Although as Byrne says (1975, p. 7).

Until the inexorable pattern of lower take-up by girls of scientific and technical school and later college examinations is reversed, there cannot be a flow of suitably qualified women candidates for teaching posts in colleges and polytechnics other than for domestic and welfare subjects.

Yet, this is far from being the only reason why women are so noticeably absent from the academic staff of institutions of higher education. Overt discrimination on grounds of sex in relation to employment is now illegal in Britain, but the onus is on those who have been discriminated against to supply evidence of this to an industrial tribunal.[55] This has proved difficult enough in many cases, but in relation to academic employment it may be almost impossible. If a number of equivalently qualified candidates are short-listed for a post, it would be very difficult to prove that a woman amongst them had been discriminated against by not being employed, even if this was the case.

Women may be discriminated against in applying for academic posts on a variety of grounds. As already suggested, their choice of postgraduate work may have been in an area which is regarded as having low status within the discipline. They may be considered as bad employment 'risks' on the grounds that they may leave to get married, or to have children, after only a short time. Academic employment for females may be seen by male academics on appointment committees as something which contravenes the ideology of the sexual division of labour in industrial societies. Also, as Blackstone and Fulton argue, women may lack academic 'sponsors' who take responsibility for furthering their academic career from postgraduate days onwards, because most networks of sponsors are composed of males, and there are fewer female academics to act as sponsors to postgraduate students.[56]

Other factors are also influential in the failure of women to obtain academic posts. Fewer women than men actually apply for posts, and this is not only because the 'pool' of women candidates is smaller, but also because women, particularly if they are married, or are expected to care for dependent relatives, may have a restricted choice of work area.[57] Lack of confidence may also prevent women from applying for posts which they are capable of taking up. And child-rearing may make full-time posts difficult to manage, so that married women may tend to apply only for part-time posts.

Even for women who are successful in obtaining academic posts, all problems do not immediately disappear. Promotion may be difficult to obtain, either because women academics are sometimes less qualified than male academics (with fewer completed PhDs and first class honours degrees) or because they have fewer publications.[58] Blackstone and Fulton found that women academics in both Britain and America tend to have higher teaching loads than male colleagues (which may help to prevent them publishing as much as men), and a higher

103

commitment to teaching.[59] But the same study also noted that women are less often involved in postgraduate teaching than men, an area of work which often forms an important criterion of promotion.[60]

Because there are so few women holding tenured, full-time posts in universities or polytechnics, and even fewer in senior positions, women are often effectively excluded from positions of power and authority within those institutions. Universities and polytechnics are highly bureaucratic, with complex hierarchies of authority.[61] Although Moodie and Eustace, in their extensive study of British universities, argue that during this century non-professorial staff have seen a substantial increase in the amount of power that they wield in relation to professorial and lay-persons, their own analysis still suggests otherwise.[62] And if ordinary lecturers have begun to gain power in universities at the expense of other groups, it is male lecturers rather than female lecturers who have become thus privileged, in contradistinction to the arguments of those who claim that these days *everyone* holds power in universities:[63]

> Firstly the junior academics united . . . and successfully invaded the faculty boards, senates and councils. Then the impossible happened; the universities had to bow to the participation of students in their most sacred places. The last class interest group emerging is the ultimate proletariat of technicians, clerical and maintenance workers. We shall soon find them in our professorial appointments committees.

Women academics in part-time, temporary or marginal posts are indeed likely to have an even less certain place in the bureaucratic hierarchy than cleaners, students or porters, all of whom enjoy some status and relative permanency within their institutions. Because women are under-represented as teachers in higher education, their chances of influencing bureaucratic processes of decision-making — whether these refer to matters of curriculum, budgeting, facilities, resources, admissions policies or appointments — are only good if they are prepared to acquiesce to the decisions of their male colleagues.

Further, as is the case for women students, there is often

cultural exclusion of women academics from potentially important learning situations participated in by their male colleagues.[64] This applies not only to intellectual discussion, but also to other important aspects of academic life and work; political in-fighting, and preparation for formal decision-making take place not in committee rooms or senate chambers, but in senior common room bars, at football matches or over rounds of golf. The formal workings of bureaucracies often seek merely to confirm what has already been decided somewhere else by somebody or other. Since women are rarely included or welcomed into the male cultural world of beer-drinking or port-sipping, sexual innuendo, team-sports and shoulder-slapping, they are effectively prevented from acquiring the kind of inside knowledge of how their institutions work which is so essential to meaningful participation in bureaucratic systems. And as Whitehead has shown for a very different but comparable setting, women who try to enter the closed cultural world of men are likely to meet with considerable ridicule and resistance.[65] She says (1976, p. 201):

> Much of the behaviour I have described is not by any means confined to other places, other times, another class.
> . . . Men's drinking groups occur in senior common rooms, the Houses of Parliament, the Inns of Court, Board Rooms, recreation clubs and in pubs, bars and clubs with a variety of clientele.

There are, then, not only very few women actually employed as academics in higher education, but it is also the case that this group suffers from the problem of tokenism. That is, there are too few women in the power-structure of higher education for them to be able to make much impact on the basic assumptions, sexism, and discriminatory practices of many of their male colleagues. Further, there are not enough women academics in a position to help female undergraduates and graduate students not to underrate their own potential achievements, and to encourage these students to endeavour to become academics themselves. And so the cycle of discrimination and female 'dropping-out' is perpetuated, not only by the subject choices of girls at school and in higher-education, but also by the very absence of sufficient women in the academic hierarchies to help their sisters onto the ladder of academe.

Academic Freedom and Women in Higher Education

It seems evident from the foregoing analysis that women remain seriously under-represented in higher education, both as students and as teachers or researchers, and that consequently many women are still failing to achieve their full academic potential. Even for those women who are successful, the hegemony of male culture and the sexism inherent in many disciplines and in the 'hidden curriculum' of higher education, prevent them from doing as well as they might in a different cultural and curricular context.

More women will only get into higher education if they begin to study at school the disciplines like the sciences and technology which have traditionally been seen as 'masculine' or if, alternatively, entry requirements for higher education become more flexible, so that all subjects can be studied with a minimum of previous background in a particular discipline.[66] At the level of undergraduate study, discrimination against female applicants is probably lower than it has ever been, following the Sex Discrimination Act, but if girls continue to compete against themselves for increasingly limited places on arts and social sciences courses, then the absence of overt discrimination will be of no help. The curriculum of higher education must also become less sexist, or women who are successful in obtaining places will find little to hold their interest and attention once they are there. More efforts must be made to make procedures for applying for postgraduate places and academic appointments less amenable to discrimination against women on grounds of sex, or the 'wastage' of women at the graduate and postgraduate stages of higher education will continue. The more women there are in higher education at every level, the greater will be the possibility of the male cultural hegemony being overthrown, and the less will be the extent to which institutions of higher education reproduce the ideological supports of the sexual division of labour in the social relations of production.

The implications of the struggles now being fought for and by women in higher education go far beyond the system itself. They involve re-examining many assumptions, values and principles which underlie Britain's present way of life and capitalist mode of production. In recognizing and demanding

106

that everyone has a right to enter higher education if they wish, and that they also have a right to be taught in a non-sexist way, women are not only putting forward their own cause, but the whole question of social justice. Some male students and academics in higher education may see the entry of larger numbers of women and non-sexist knowledge as a threat to their academic freedom. But sexism in higher education is a misuse of freedom and of power; men have no right to academic freedom if its very existence denies freedom to women.

Chapter 5

Women as Teachers - Separate and Unequal?

The major concern of the argument put forward so far has been to suggest that both the family and the educational system are instrumental in reproducing the existing sexual and class divisions of labour in capitalist British society. Hence, girls from working-class families (despite undergoing state secondary schooling until the age of sixteen), are likely to enter the same low-paid, unskilled jobs once done by their mothers, and eventually to become housewives and mothers themselves. Although changes have occurred within the education system, the structure of capitalist society remains essentially the same. By concentrating girls in areas of subject specialization inappropriate to other than traditional 'women's jobs', schools ensure that monotonous, insecure, badly paid jobs, and the unpaid work of domestic labour and childcare continue to be carried out by women. Girls from middle-class families would seem, on the face of it, to have more opportunities open to them than working-class girls. However, although middle-class girls may remain at school longer, and achieve a higher measure of academic success than their working-class counterparts, and although there is more expectation that they will enter some kind of career (perhaps combining this with marriage and a family), their options are, no less than those of working-class girls, channelled into areas traditionally occupied by women. Teaching has been an occupation entered by women in large numbers; in the nineteenth century mainly working-class or lower middle-class women, but this century increasingly middle-class only. And like secretarial or office-work, or nursing, teaching has promised more to the women entering it than it has actually given them, in terms of status, financial rewards and career prospects. In this chapter it will be suggested that women who enter teaching have been no less strongly socialized into accepting the existing sexual division of labour than have other women. Because of this the position of most women in teaching is one which emphasizes the distinctive place of women in the sexual division of labour, as will become apparent in the ensuing analysis.

It has been implicitly recognized for some time that teaching, because it recruits large numbers of women and because it has so many internal divisions, is, therefore, a profession which differs from other professional occupations such as medicine or law; it is highly bureaucratic, has low status, little autonomy over clients or practice of the occupation, and no definite knowledge base.[1] Indeed, in the nineteenth century employers of teachers in elementary schools were anxious to exert strong social control over their employees, both in their teaching and in their private lives.[2] Salaries of teachers remained low at that time because as Turner (1974, p. 31) notes, employers 'were inclined to believe that teachers, like their pupils, should not be encouraged to seek a higher status than that to which they were born'. Nevertheless, some educationalists have argued that teaching is one of the few occupations which has provided women with the chance of social mobility independent of a man[3] and has also offered them the possibility of taking up a well-paid occupation with high job satisfaction and excellent career prospects.[4] However, it will be argued here that since the nineteenth century women teachers have traditionally been engaged in teaching at a lower level and with younger pupils than have men teachers, and that they have been differentially rewarded financially and in terms of status, as compared to their male colleagues.[5] If teaching has provided some women with an opening into a professional career, it has done so without fundamentally changing the position of those women in the sexual division of labour in British society.

Teaching as a Feminine Activity

Recently there has been much interest shown in the links between families and schools as institutions which together contribute towards the reproduction of class relationships and the sexual division of labour in capitalist societies.[6] Families and schools in such societies share the responsibility for rearing and socializing children, and it has been further suggested that there is an analogy between the way that the family deals with children and the manner in which schools treat them.[7] This affects not only the socialization and education of girls but may also be seen to influence how women teachers teach, what they teach and how they are perceived of as teachers. Our present sexual division of labour demands that women work mainly outside the dominant system of production and the labour market, undertaking domestic labour and rearing children within the context of the nuclear family. Primary and nursery school teaching require many of the same skills and involve confrontation of similar problems to those found in child-rearing. That there is a similarity between motherhood and the teaching of young children is something understood by teachers and by student teachers[8] as much as by parents. As Gibson (1970–1, p. 23) says, 'there is general agreement that the primary school teacher should be more concerned to act as a sort of substitute mother than the secondary school teacher'. Although the establishment by some local educational authorities of middle schools, which are intermediate between primary and secondary schools, has blurred the distinction between the primary and secondary sectors as separate spheres of education, nevertheless a strong distinction is still made in teaching between those who teach young children and those who teach older children. Generally speaking, the older the pupils, the greater the status of those who teach them.[9] Whereas the task of teaching young children is thought to be mainly concerned with inculcating acceptable standards of behaviour, teaching basic skills and encouraging pupils to accept the value of learning, the task of teaching older children is seen to focus on the instruction of pupils and evaluation of what has been learnt.[10] Despite the existence of middle schools, the findings of Cortis's research on the differences between primary and secondary schools are still of relevance to the argument that the teaching of young children differs from the teaching of older children.[11] Cortis (1972–3, p. 113) says:

> the primary teacher . . . appears a more 'rigid', insensitive type coming from a more densely populated area, with overtones of 'suspiciousness' and 'conventionality' distinguishing his [*sic*] behaviour. The secondary teacher, on the other hand, is more 'sensitive', more satisfied with his work, and has more progressive educational attitudes than his primary counterpart. He is less 'rigid', even inclined to 'laxity' and has more commitment to his academic main subject as a separate identity.

Implicit in the distinctions made between the teaching of young children and the teaching of older children is the idea that, whereas the former task is most suited to women, the latter is the province of male teachers. For many years a major teachers' union, the National Association of Schoolmasters, believed that boys over the age of seven should be taught mainly by men, although the Sex Discrimination Act has now made this belief difficult to sustain.[12] The Association in question was originally a splinter group from the National Union of Teachers, breaking away in 1919 when the NUT took up the cause of equal pay for women teachers. Hence, there is a clear link between anti-feminist beliefs and the idea that women are only capable of teaching young children. Although the NAS has now amalgamated with the Union of Women Teachers, this in no way diminishes its anti-feminist stance during much of this century, although the amalgamation does indicate a grudging willingness to recognize the equal contribution of some women in teaching.

Until the Second World War it was also believed that once women were married their new domestic roles meant that they were unable to continue teaching other people's children, so that women teachers who married were sacked from their posts. Secondary education itself was for a long time the preserve of the church and clerics, so that it became associated with men as teachers long before industrialization, and even after industrialization, it was only in the twentieth century that more than a few privileged girls were able to gain access to a secondary education. Both of these factors meant that secondary teaching was historically associated with men rather than women, and this association, backed up by our societal division of labour, has remained ever since.[13]

Bowles and Gintis have argued that schools in capitalist society mirror the authority relationships found in the wider society, so that pupils are imbued with a sense of hierarchy and a set of values appropriate to their eventual place in that hierarchy once they leave school.[14] There is, indeed, more than one sense in which relationships in schools replicate those found in the wider society. For example, maternalistic and pastoral roles are often played by women teachers, and paternalistic and authoritarian roles by men teachers. Many primary schools implicitly recognize the similarity between their relationships and structure, and that of the family, even referring to their organization of pupils as 'family' groupings. Mothers are frequently seen as the model for teachers of young children and fathers seen as the model for teachers of older children.[15] Hence, although some aspects of teaching are considered appropriate tasks for women, other aspects are considered unsuitable.

Women Teachers: Financial Rewards and Career Chances

The concept of teaching as a feminine role in relation to certain kinds of learning and particular age ranges of pupils is fundamental to an understanding of the position which women occupy within teaching. Despite entering it in large numbers for many decades, and despite the achievement of feminist victories over the employment of married women teachers and equal pay, as a group women in teaching have never achieved as much in financial or career terms as have men. Once they stray outside the confines of primary education they may find themselves unable to obtain promotion or forced to adopt stereotyped roles. For example, in a study of a large comprehensive school, Richardson found that whereas the head of the school was seen to play a paternal role towards the pupils, the senior mistress was allocated responsibility for pastoral care – a role which might make further career development difficult.[16]

When we examine the distribution of senior teaching posts,

we find that in both primary and secondary schools men are proportionately more likely to hold positions as head teachers than are women (see Table 5.1).[17] Even the Plowden Report on Primary Schooling, whilst recognizing the predominance of women over men as primary school teachers, nevertheless entitled one section of its report, 'The Head Teacher and *his* staff'.[18]

TABLE 5.1 *Full-time teachers by grade of post, England and Wales, all maintained schools, 1974*

| | Primary | | Secondary | |
	Men	Women	Men	Women
Head teachers	13,565	10,215	4,386	1,046
Deputy heads	7,092	10,788	4,329	2,382
2nd masters/mistresses	22	47	906	1,757
Senior teachers	–	–	2,403	496
Scale 5	48	28	14,491	3,600
Scale 4	774	1,096	26,209	11,267
Scale 3	6,764	13,597	21,688	15,647
Scale 2	8,796	36,251	19,136	20,257
Scale 1	8,606	76,390	24,646	35,224
Total	45,667	148,412	118,194	91,676

Source: DES Statistics of Education 1974, vol. 4, *Teachers*, Table 23, pp. 42-5.

From Table 5.1 we can see that not only are men more likely than women to have posts as headteachers, but also that they are to be found in greater proportion in senior posts of all kinds, with the exception of deputy-heads in primary schools. In the year to which the table refers, over 80 per cent of female primary school teachers held posts of Scale three or below, but this was the case for only just over 50 per cent of male primary teachers. In secondary schools the position was similar, with about 40 per cent of male teachers in posts of Scale four or above, but only 20 per cent of female teachers in comparable jobs. This is partly a reflection of the fact that more women than men leave the occupation before they have had sufficient teaching experience to be promoted to senior posts as is shown in Table 5.2. Nevertheless women who do remain in full-time teaching are, on the whole, less likely to gain promotion than their male colleagues.

TABLE 5.2 *Age structure of full-time teachers, maintained schools, England and Wales, 1973-4*

	Under 25	25–34	35–44	45–54	55–59	60 & over	Total
Men in service April 1973	10,277	56,214	36,047	31,048	13,212	10,104	156,902
All men leavers March 1974	987	3,953	1,279	753	404	2,770	10,146
Women in service April 1973	35,151	76,515	51,581	40,513	15,059	9,229	228,048
All women leavers by March 1974	4,480	14,071	3,065	1,730	852	3,445	27,643

Source: DES Statistics of Education 1974, vol. 4, *Teachers*, Table 20 p. 32.

However, if part-time posts in teaching are examined, it becomes apparent that many of these are held by women rather than by men. In January 1974 there were 40,873 qualified part-time women teachers in maintained secondary, middle and primary schools in the United Kingdom, but only 6,501 male part-timers.[19] Part-time teachers are amongst the most disadvantaged in the occupation. Paid only for the hours they teach, and not for preparation or marking, they receive no holiday pay, sick pay or maternity pay, are liable to dismissal at a week's notice, and possess no security of employment from the end of one academic year to the beginning of the next. Only those teaching sixteen or more hours a week are entitled to any protection under the Employment Protection Act.[20] But since the family and the school are so effective in reproducing the existing social relations of production and ensuring that the sexual division of labour remains unchanged, it is not surprising that many women are forced to take up part-time employment in teaching. Carrying out domestic labour, rearing young children and other responsibilities within the nuclear family are tasks that, if given only to women, may well not be compatible with full time teaching. Unfortunately, the convenience of teaching part-time is not matched by the conditions and terms of employment which this kind of work offers.

Not only are most women in teaching placed in inferior posts when compared to their male colleagues, but they are also disadvantaged in salary terms at almost every level of the occupation, despite the existence of equal pay in teaching since 1960.

If teaching, then, does provide an occupation for women which has good pay, career prospects and high status, it does so only in comparison with other jobs for women, which also reflect the existing sexual division of labour in society. Men who enter teaching have a much greater likelihood of receiving high salaries and promotion than most of their female colleagues (see Table 5.3). Their involvement in marriage and the nuclear family is seldom held to be detrimental to their careers, whilst this is often evidenced as a reason why women make unreliable teachers, are thus not promoted, and are paid less. The contribution of men to this unreliability is seldom recognized by those who thus criticize women teachers.

TABLE 5.3 *Average salaries, all teachers in maintained schools in England and Wales, 1974*

Type of school	Qualification	Men	Women
Primary	Graduate	£2419	£2071
Primary	Non-graduate	£2743	£2010
Primary	All teachers	£2467	£2013
Secondary	Graduate	£2755	£2399
Secondary	Non-graduate	£2387	£2071
Secondary	All teachers	£2548	£2184

Source: DES Statistics of Education 1974, vol. 4, *Teachers*, Table 24, pp. 46–7.

The Commitment of Women to Teaching

It has sometimes been claimed that women teachers do not display the same degree of commitment to their occupation as that shown by men teachers.[21] This lesser commitment is explained in the same terms as women's inferior salaries and career structures, with reference to the 'real' interests of women in marriage and the nuclear family rather than in work. Hoyle (1969, pp. 87–8) for example talks of:

> the 'special conditions' attaching to female employment such as the fact that their careers are often intermittent, that they are usually only secondary breadwinners in the family, that they tend to be residentially immobile.

Hoyle, of course, assumes that all female teachers are married, earning less than their husbands, and willing to cease paid employment on child-birth. Furthermore, there is the implicit assumption that all these factors are the fault of women and are not attributable to their relationship with men in the sexual division of labour, or to the manner in which capitalist societies organize and reward productive and non-productive work.

Other writers have referred to the higher rate of 'wastage' amongst women teachers leaving the occupation, as compared to men teachers. In 1967 the Plowden Report noted that three women in primary schools left to every one man, although this does not take into account the much smaller number of men in primary teaching to begin with.[22] Pollard suggests that the wastage rate amongst women teachers is so high that we must see women in the occupation as the least professional and most expensively trained members.[23] Talking about the campaign launched during the 1960s to encourage married women to return to teaching, Pollard (1974, p. 57) recalls that this raised questions about 'dilution of the profession, and about where the priorities of a married woman might lie if, say, her children were ill'. Again, blame is attached to individual women, and not to the system of social relations of production which ensure that it is usually married women – not married men – who have to care for sick children.

In any case, it is not justifiable to assume that because women often have heavy responsibilities for carrying out domestic labour and caring for children, their commitment to any other task is necessarily lower than that of men. Even if women do give up teaching to have children, many are anxious to return to teaching as soon as they are able to do so.[24] In a study of student teachers Hellawell and Smithers found that, whereas the future career ambitions of male students often lay outside schoolteaching or education altogether (1973-4, p. 46), 'women students were consistently more favourably disposed towards actual schoolteaching than men'. Women in this study were thus found to possess a greater commitment to teaching than men.[25]

Grace's analysis of teacher role conflict found that women were less likely to experience most areas of role conflict, and showed a tendency to tolerate more inconsistencies in their occupation than did most of the men.[26] He does not comment that this may be merely a reflection of women's lives in contemporary capitalist societies which typically contain more contradictions and inconsistencies than do most men's lives. And although Grace tries to argue that women's lesser perception of role conflict is indicative of their smaller degree of commitment to their occupation, this assumption would seem to hinge on a definition of commitment – something which Grace himself recognizes to be balanced delicately between advancement in a career through constant mobility from school to school, and remaining in one school but showing strong commitment to the pupils in that establishment. In the latter respect women in Grace's research shared loyalty to their schools and pupils with less than 10 per cent of them showing strong desire for career advancement. As one said (Grace, 1972, p. 74): 'Being a married woman it is not so important for me to "get on" – I want to know a group of children – "getting on" is secondary.' Indeed, the greater degree of constraint operating on the circumstances and locations in which women teachers (if they are married or have dependents) have to find jobs, may indicate that they are much more persistent and committed to teaching than many men, particularly since it is still a strongly-held cultural assumption that whilst a woman moves with her husband if the latter acquires a new job, the reverse is seldom acceptable.[27]

Women and Teacher Training

It has been suggested that certain kinds of teaching are recognized as areas of feminine expertise, whereas other areas are

seen as more appropriate to male skills. These beliefs, which
are based on the traditional sexual division of labour found in
capitalist societies, have a serious effect on the status, salary
and careers of many women teachers. But it is not only the
school and the family which reproduce the sexual division of
labour; the process of teacher training also has a part to play.
Indeed, teacher training as a form of vocational preparation
separate from any other form of education was something
which was partly, if not entirely, set up with women in mind.
In the nineteenth century when colleges began to be established specifically for the training of teachers, few women
who wished to teach were able to enter the occupation as
men were, through the church or a university education.[28]
For those women who entered teaching after a period at
training college, as Parry and Parry (1974, p. 172) note:

> Sexual divisions between training colleges for men and
> women respectively were rigidly institutionalised. The
> connection between religious and moral training, and the
> notion of the enforcement of sexual morals, which formed
> such a central theme of the Victorian era, was manifested
> in colleges organized more on the model of the religious
> seminary.

Not only were there rigid sexual divisions in the provision
of training places, but strong lay, church and community
control was exercised over both the work and social lives of
teachers once they commenced work, and this remained the
case throughout the nineteenth century.[29] However, women
who wished to enter teaching as an escape from the even
more restricting life of a spinster or that of a domestic ser-
vant, had little choice but to accept these social controls over
trainee and practising teachers. Training of women for teaching in special colleges was considered more necessary than the
training of men, and heads of secondary schools often preferred to recruit male teachers from university or ecclesiasti-
cal sources.[30]
The courses which women at training college in the nineteenth century underwent were often more concerned with
reinforcing the traditional skills and characteristics associated with being feminine, than with offering instruction in the
professional skills of teaching. Domestic economy formed an

118

important facet of the education provided, both on the grounds that women would have to teach it and that they would need to know how to run their own homes later.[31] Discipline was strict and students were rarely allowed out of college either alone or accompanied by other students; they were forced to wear similar clothes and exercise often consisted of walking in a crocodile or military-style drill.[32] The harsh conditions and social control relaxed a little towards the end of the century, the quality of training improved and some day training colleges, as opposed to residential ones, were set up.

But despite these and many other changes[33] which have subsequently taken place in teacher training since the end of the last century, much of the original ideology of training colleges remains. Women training as teachers are still seen differently from men similarly training, and for a long time, even in the recent decades of this century, they have been subject to a social control based on assumptions about the subordinate status of women in society. Training colleges retained rules about the behaviour and conduct of their students long after many universities and other similar institutions had begun to relax those following the period of student unrest in the late 1960s. Indeed, it is not so many years since a student at a college of education was asked to terminate her course after having been found in her college room with a man 'after hours', on the grounds that a girl with such loose standards of sexual morality was unsuited to the teaching of other peoples' children. It is difficult to imagine a similar misdemeanour by a male student being tackled or seen in the same way. There is a curious, almost ironic, contradiction in the beliefs held about women as student or practising teachers, in that their training constantly emphasizes to them their proper place in the sexual division of labour, and their ultimate destiny as wives and mothers, whilst at the same time expecting them to behave as though they were asexual.

It is not only that teacher training emphasizes to women, and is effective in reproducing, the existing sexual division of labour in society. Its task in this respect has been made easier by the relative spatial and educational isolation of teacher training from other forms of higher and further education, an isolation which was commented upon unfavourably by the

James Report in 1972, and which was seen by that Report as a major contributory factor to the divisiveness existing in teaching as an occupation.[34] The geographical isolation of many colleges has allowed them to function effectively as social controllers of the skills and behaviour of their mostly female students. Indeed, Taylor says of training colleges before the Second World War that they were often institutions (1969, p. 205)

> in which a diluted form of gracious living was engaged in by a largely spinster staff, in an impressive if educationally unsuitable and draughty building at the end of a mile-long drive, ten miles from the nearest town.

Although there are probably no colleges now which conform to this stereotype, legacies of those days remain in teacher training. The academic isolation of many establishments and their preparation of students for a relatively narrow vocational field has, intentionally or not, limited the occupational horizons of many of those students. Girls in particular, have often entered teacher training not because they especially wish to teach, but because they have not acquired the qualifications for entry to any other form of higher education. But the subsequent certification which they have obtained from colleges of education has frequently had no currency outside the education sector. Certainly, cut-backs in initial teacher training and the consequent mergers of colleges of education with other institutions of further and higher education, have had the effect of increasing the range and diversity of courses offered, but this has come too late for many women, and it is a policy which has been carried out at the expense of those colleges which have been closed altogether.

Teacher training of non-graduates in isolation from other students undergoing higher education then, has contributed to the reproduction of the existing social relations of production in society, and has reinforced — or even to some extent created — the ideology that the teaching of young children is a feminine vocation, whilst the teaching of older children belongs to a different category of skill altogether, to be prepared for, in the main, by taking a degree first, and teacher training later. The present enthusiasm for recruiting into secondary schools teachers with industrial or commercial experience may only serve to strengthen those beliefs and exclude yet more women teachers from the world of teaching beyond the primary or middle school.[35]

Women as Teachers: are they Different?

There is certainly evidence to indicate that women teachers are socialized into believing that their vocation is to teach young children. But are women, as teachers, really so different from men teachers? Or is this just a myth which helps to perpetuate the existing ideology and structure of the sexual division of labour in society? There are certainly those who believe that women do teach in a way very different from that of men. Morrison and McIntyre (1969, p. 51) for example, claim that:

> The sex of teachers is a factor which appears to have an equally pervasive influence on classroom relationships; among other things, it has been shown to affect the teacher's perception of pupils, the aspirations and achievements of pupils, and the teacher's degree of involvement in the job of teaching.

But, on the other hand, in his investigations into formal and informal teaching styles, Bennett found few marked differences of opinion or teaching aims between male and female teachers[36] and discovered only a small amount of evidence to suggest that informal teaching styles were favoured more by men than by women.[37]

But there is material which implies that women teachers in mixed schools, especially secondary schools, may experience more discipline problems than men teachers in a comparable situation. In a series of interview with new teachers, a teacher in her probationary year studied by Hannam, Smith and Stephenson (1976, p. 63), said of her pupils in a comprehensive school:

> if only they were scared of me so that they would sit in their places and be quiet and listen and do what I say . . . I can't do it the way the kids are used to because I'm not a big aggressive male, you see.

Other female students in the same study reported particular problems with their boy pupils, sometimes calling in other, male, members of staff to help.[38] On occasions, pupils themselves would suggest this as a solution, as one woman explained (Hannam *et al.*, 1976, p. 78):

> I don't hit boys who mess around. . . . If I don't hit them the others get very cross and uptight, 'Miss, can't you shut them up? Get the slipper out and hit them. Send them to Mr Pendry, he'll hit them'.

That these discipline problems were caused as much by the sexist stereotypes already possessed by the pupils as by any fault of the teachers concerned, is evidenced elsewhere in the same work, where female teachers complain of sexual banter and abuse from male pupils, even in primary schools.[39] And this is one of the problems that confronts female teachers; the schools in which they teach are busy socializing their pupils into the existing sexual division of labour, so that boys in particular, as they grow older, are likely to assume power over women teachers and exploit it. Indeed children may not see women as effective teachers at all. Musgrove and Taylor (1969, pp. 26–7) found that:

> children's stereotype of the good teacher is a young married man with children, who gives little homework and no corporal punishment. They may reject as 'good' teachers women, elderly teachers, and those inclined to behave towards them as their parents might.

Dale's research on mixed and single-sex schools found that girls showed a preference for male teachers, and that female teachers, especially those in single-sex schools, were often seen as unpleasant, harsh disciplinarians, obsessed by trivial details and academic work.[40] Dale himself intimates that women teachers may experience discipline problems and claims, further, that (1969, p. 95):

> there is a possibility that the female personality may not be ideally suited to the traditional class teaching situation . . . where there is some need for dominance, which comes more naturally to a man than a woman.

This assumption, of course, begs the question of whether it is women *per se* who cannot teach mixed classes of secondary school age, or of whether it is the way that women are socialized, the way that their pupils are socialized and the social relationships of production in society and their accompanying ideology which makes both women teachers and their pupils unable to believe that they *can* cope.

There is insufficient evidence for it to be possible to decide whether, in fact, all women do teach differently from all men. In so far as existing data support this conclusion, it is arguable that the differences observed may be due less to the actual abilities and skills of female teachers as compared with male teachers, than to the sexual division of labour and its ideological supports as they exist in capitalist societies.

Women, Unions and Teacher Politics

Sexual divisions in teaching have not been confined to teaching or to teacher training only, but have also permeated the arena of teacher politics and unionization. Since the nineteenth century secondary school teachers have had separate unions for male and female teachers, although the National Union of Teachers has always admitted teachers of both sexes to membership. The National Association of Schoolmasters, which grew out of a split with the NUT over the issue of equal pay for women, maintained for many decades of this century that any teaching union which attempted to represent both male and female members was doomed to failure as the two groups had contradictory interests. Men, it was argued, saw teaching as a career and major source of income which was poorly rewarded in comparison to other 'male' jobs. On the other hand, it was claimed, women saw teaching as a job, not a career, and comparing it with other occupations open to them, found it satisfactory in most respects, including salaries. Subsequently the NAS has joined forces with the Union of Women Teachers, and so has been forced to partially retract its earlier arguments about women teachers. However, the UWT sees itself as an association of 'career-teachers', and not simply as a union for all women in teaching, and with the NAS, and the NUT, has been one of the most militant of the teacher associations in pursuit of salary claims and improved conditions of work.[41] The NUT, which has a two-thirds female membership, has often been a staunch defender of the interests of women teachers, although its Executive Committee has usually contained a predominance of males.[42] Other teacher associations with women members, for instance the Association of Assistant Mistresses and the Headmistresses Association, have followed their male counterparts in being less militant in their demands over salaries and work conditions, and have concerned themselves with other, more 'professional' aspects of teaching.[43]

In so far as the interests of women and men teachers do differ, the differences can be seen to stem more from the structure of capitalist society than from any other single factor. If women were not seen as subordinate to men, and expected to engage primarily in domestic labour and child-rearing within the context of the nuclear family, then the interests of *all* women teachers in teacher politics might show a greater coalescence with those of men than they do at present. Zeigler, writing about American teachers, has even suggested that the existence of a large number of women and a smaller number of men in teaching may cause men's political activities and interests to become 'feminised'. His reasoning is that teaching is an occupation best suited to females who are usually satisfied with it as a job, who hold more orthodox political views than men, and who are unlikely to become embroiled in militant politics; he tries to provide data which demonstrate that men in teaching may be forced to adopt similar strategies if they wish to remain teachers.[44]

Certainly, the failure of women to participate fully in white-collar unions is an established sociological proposition about union activity.[45] But women in the NUT over the last hundred years, have supported the late nineteenth- and early twentieth-century Suffragette Movement, pursued the issue of equal pay for over forty years until its achievement in teaching in 1960 and fought hard for the removal of the ban on the employment of married teachers. The Union of Women Teachers has been a more recent arrival on the scene of teacher politics, but since the late 1960s has shown as much militancy as other unions in supporting various forms of direct action on pay claims and conditions of work.[46]

Teacher associations with women members have not always tried hard to interest most of their members in full and active participation, preferring instead to stress the instrumental benefits of membership such as third party insurance or sick pay schemes.[47] But, in addition, women have from an early age been socialized into accepting a position in the social relations of production which isolates and excludes them from direct participation in class struggle or any other form of political action, a position which places them predomi-nantly in non-productive roles within the nuclear family and emphasizes their different role in the division of labour as compared to men. In recent years most teachers who have taken strike action or supported militant sanctions have been men rather than women.[48] But this can only be explained partially in terms of the different interests of male and female teachers. Indeed, women's lack of militancy may be partly attributable to their concern with the professional *status* of their occupation, over and above instrumental interests in salaries and conditions of work. Militant action is seen by some women teachers — and indeed by some male teachers — as a strategy which is potentially very damaging to the professional status of their occupation.[49] But the spread of the Women's Movement in Britain has been particularly strong amongst those involved in education, and this is likely to ensure that in future women teachers become more poli-tically active, both inside and outside their occupational associations.

Women as Teachers: Separate and Unequal

In this chapter the status, role and career prospects of women teachers have been examined in some detail. It has been sug-gested that women who teach are both seen as, and see them-selves, differently from, men teachers, in terms of the kind of teaching to which they are suited, their commitment to their occupation, and their involvement in teacher politics. This separation is encouraged and shaped by both the socialization of women within the family and their education, as well as by the social relations of production, in particular the sexual division of labour existing in capitalist societies which socialization and education help to reproduce. Women in this division of labour are seen primarily as domestic, non-productive labourers within the context of the nuclear family, who are expected to have responsibility for the rearing of children. The teaching of young children by women is seen as not incompatible with the sexual division of labour, but women who teach beyond this level may be seen as intruding into a male preserve, may be perceived by their pupils as unsatisfactory teachers and may experience discipline problems. In all types of state schools, the majority of senior posts and headships are held by men rather than by women, and the promotion prospects and financial rewards offered to female teachers are less good than those available to male teachers.[50] Women are assumed to be less committed to teaching than men, but it is often the other tasks which they are expected to fulfil within the nuclear family, and their subordinate status as wage-earners in relation to men, which gives rise to a lesser commitment, or a commitment to a particular school rather than rapid career advancement. In training for teaching women often follow a different path from men, and their geographical and academic isolation may subject them to sexist processes during their training, whilst the qualifications which they obtain severely limit their career opportunities. In teacher politics, women are often less active than men, although they have fought hard to achieve victory on issues of special interest to them. As with their level of commitment, their non-involvement in union activities is as much due to their position in the sexual division of labour and their exclusion from the politics of class struggle, as to their own lack of interest.

Since the nineteenth century teaching has provided an apparently excellent escape route for women seeking financial and social independence from the nuclear family. But in reality the escape has often been illusory. Women in teaching have, to a considerable degree, been confined to the same roles and skills that they are expected to fulfil within the home and in the family, and their status in relation to male teachers has remained subordinate. Despite the existence of equal pay and the passing of a Sex Discrimination Act, women in teaching do not occupy a position similar to that occupied by men. They remain separate, and unequal.

Chapter 6

Women, Education and Society:

the Possibilities of Change

It has been suggested in this book that the education of women in British society is frequently different from, and sometimes inferior to, the education received by men in the same society. There are clearly many aspects of education in both schools and in institutions of higher and further education which require change if women are to develop their full potential in schooling and other areas of educational opportunity. However, blame for the present inequalities of the education of women in Britain cannot be laid solely at the door of educational establishments, educationists and educational policy makers; the capitalist mode of production, the family, and the role of women in the sexual division of labour are also crucial factors. If sexism and sex-stereotyping are to disappear from society, and if the positions of women and men in the sexual division of labour are to be changed to such an extent that labour is no longer allocated on the basis of gender, then it cannot be expected that change in education alone will achieve these goals. Changes will also need to be made in the wider society, in the allocation of responsibility for child care and domestic labour, in roles and relationships within the family, in the relative statures attached to manual and mental labour. But this is not to say that changes in education will have no significant impact on society, since a reduction in the degree of sexism and sexual differentiation in education will also help to increase people's awareness of the possibility of achieving change elsewhere in society.

Education and the Eradication of Sexism

One of the biggest threats to the reduction of sexism in education is that posed by fluctuations in the economy. Economic recessions, like the one experienced by Britain in the 1970s, can result in pressures for, and policies on, cuts in public expenditure. Since education in British society is a major area of expenditure, it is particularly vulnerable to public spending cuts. Although it may be argued that people's attitudes are of crucial importance to the existence or absence of sexism in schools, differentiation on grounds of sex is often based on unequal allocation and distribution of learning resources. Furthermore, sexism may be implicit in certain kinds of resources, such as reading materials or textbooks. If expenditure in schools is cut back, sexist reading schemes and other sexist literature may continue to be used, simply because non-sexist replacements are too expensive to purchase.[1] Indeed, people may be discouraged from producing non-sexist literature because there is only a limited market for it. Children in primary schools may be forced to use play equipment which encourages sex-stereotyping because schools cannot afford to buy sufficient equipment for all children to choose which they use on the basis of interest. In secondary schools, shortages of money may mean that girls continue to be unable to make non-traditional choices of subject, such as sciences, technical subjects or mathematics, because not enough teachers or facilities are available for this to be possible. Similarly, boys may be prevented from taking arts subjects or domestic subjects.

In higher education the closure of colleges of education may well reduce the choice of courses available to women students with arts qualifications. Government initiatives on unemployment and training of school leavers for employment may also be affecting the post-school options available to girls. In further education the Manpower Services Commission (created in 1974 to provide public employment and training services), and one of the Commission's off-shoots, the Training Services Agency, which runs training schemes and courses, have both made considerable inroads into course and curriculum development and are becoming increasingly important in the financing of higher education.[2] Since few of the people involved in the Commission or its agencies are women, and since most of the courses being provided under its auspices are technical, vocational and industrially-oriented ones which require scientific, technical or mathematical skills, girls are unlikely to benefit substantially from this involvement of the Commission in further education, and may well have their chances of taking courses suited to their interests and existing qualifications reduced. The Job Creation Scheme, which is a Government sponsored body helping to provide temporary work for the young unemployed, has also not favoured girl school leavers in its schemes, and about 76 per cent of the jobs in their programme up to 1977 were intended for boys.[3] Girl school leavers then, are likely to find their chances of continuing their education or entering a worthwhile job hampered not only by their sex and school background in arts subjects, but also by the effects of the economic recession.

Can anything be done about all this? The existing legislation on women's rights and sex discrimination does not appear to have the breadth to cope with many of these problems, partly because the procedures for making complaints are based on individual cases, whereas the problems are often general ones.[4] Furthermore, the Equal Opportunities Commission, the major official body concerned with implementing the British legislation on sex equality, has also suffered from the economic recession and the unwillingness of many to take the question of women's equality seriously in the face of what are seen as more pressing economic and political problems.[5] But there is also the further difficulty that some problems of sexism in schools seem to lie beyond the scope of legislation. Whilst it would be possible to legally require schools to provide equal resources, equipment, and teachers for both sexes, our existing educational system would make the financing of these things difficult to arrange. Under the present system of block rate-support grant allocation to local authorities by central government, it is not possible to insist that money is spent on any particular item of expenditure. And legislation on matters like sexist literature would probably be contested and opposed by teachers and teacher organisations on the grounds that the determination of what books may be used and which may not sets a dangerous precedent and threatens the autonomy of the teaching profession.

Legislation on issues of sexism and sexual differentiation is at best an incomplete answer. On other aspects of sexism in schools, such as teachers' or pupils' attitudes, legislation would not be feasible, or even conceivable.

Pressure groups of an activist kind provide another partial solution. Parent-teacher associations, women's groups both inside and outside the Women's Liberation Movement, and student or pupil groups can all agitate for a fairer allocation of resources, teachers and equipment to both boys and girls. These groups can also press for the use of non-sexist literature in schools and colleges of all kinds, by drawing up lists of what is already available and circulating these to educational establishments, and by organizing the writing of more non-sexist literature suitable for all levels and ages of students in a variety of subjects, from reading lessons to chemistry. And, of course, parents who are aware of the problems arising from sexism and sex-stereotyping can endeavour also to reduce the extent to which these processes play a part in the way their own children are brought up, so that schools which introduce sexism and sex-stereotyping are seen as deviant rather than as normal and 'natural'.

Changes in educational policy may also be advantageous to women in certain areas of schooling. For instance, the development of a core curriculum in secondary schools might help to eliminate some aspects of curricular differentiation between boys and girls. In 1976 the DES, setting out the four aspects of the then forthcoming 'Great Debate' on education, distinguished between a common curriculum in which all pupils follow the same educational pattern, and a core curriculum which suggests an irreducible minimum of subjects essential to the education of all children, with room for variation beyond that minimum.[6] Whilst noting that subjects such as English, mathematics and science might be part of this core curriculum, the document suggested that decisions about the content of a core curriculum must also take into account what subjects are already taught in secondary schools, and the needs of pupils which are being met, or that need to be met.[7] The notion of a core curriculum is a controversial issue amongst educationists, not only because of disagreements about what it should comprise, but also because of conflicts of interest over how such a curriculum could be implemented in schools without degrading the expertise and autonomy of teachers.[8] And, of course, the concept of curriculum involves more than simply what subjects are taught where. As Jenkins and Shipman point out (1976, p. 5):

> A curriculum then is concerned with prerequisites (ante-cedents, intentions), with transactions (what actually goes on in classrooms as the essential meanings are negotiated between teachers and taught, and worthwhile activities undertaken) and with outcomes (the knowledge and skill acquired by students, attitude changes, intended and un-intended side effects etc.).

Hence, to impose common subjects on schools would be in-sufficient to achieve a core curriculum, since there would also need to be agreement on common objectives.[9] However, if agreement could be reached on the many aspects of the notion of a core curriculum, to the extent that non-sexism and the teaching of basic skills (literacy, numeracy, spatial, mechanical and technical abilities) became adopted as objec-tives of secondary schooling, with an appropriate accompany-ing core of subjects, then both girls and boys would be likely to benefit. At the present time the English system of educa-tion requires an earlier degree of specialization from pupils than most other industrial societies, and elimination of some of that early specialization would reduce the chances of girls and boys leaving school with qualifications and learning back-grounds heavily dependent on a single group or category of subjects and skills.[10]

The reduction of sexism, sex stereotyping and curricular differentiation between boys and girls in schools would bene-fit both boys and girls, because it would decrease the extent to which the sexes are pushed into activities and areas of study on grounds other than personal aptitude or interest. Willis has argued that many working-class schoolboys rarely identify culturally with either academically-successful working-class boys, or with working-class girls because of the existence of two crucial cultural divisions. These divisions are, Willis claims, first the distinction between mental and manual labour, and second the division of gender.[11] The counter-school culture of some working-class boys can, Willis suggests, be seen both as a rejection of individualism and

131

mental activity, and of femininity and women as significant aspects of culture. Willis's research indicates that mental activity is often identified with both femininity and weakness, whereas manual activity is identified with masculinity, strength and virility. He says (1977, p. 149):

> If the currency of femininity were revalued, then that of mental work would have to be too. A member of the counter-school culture can only believe in the effeminacy of white collar and office work so long as wives, girlfriends and mothers are regarded as restricted, inferior and incapable of certain things.

Although non-sexist educational practices would not remove the cultural distinctions between mental and manual activity or the societal relevance of gender differences, they might reduce the significance of these divisions within schools, so that boys and girls, at least those within the same social class groupings, would come to see each other as individuals rather than as males and females.

Beyond the level of schools other changes could also be made in education. For instance, the Equal Opportunities Commission has suggested that higher and further educational institutions should make efforts in their advertisements and prospectuses to encourage women applicants.[12] In addition, institutions could become more flexible (until such time as the introduction of a core curriculum might make such flexibility less necessary), in their entrance requirements for courses. For example, the Committee of Directors of Polytechnics has set up a sub-committee investigating how much basic knowledge a student actually requires to take a degree course in science.[13] If sciences and technical subjects could be taken at post-school level by those with a variety of previous subject experiences, then the present curricular differentiation between boys and girls might be less disadvantageous to both sexes, although to some extent flexibility about previous subject knowledge already applies in the arts and social sciences. Certainly, the Open University has been successful in providing courses at degree level which require minimal knowledge of the subject taken prior to the start of the course.[14]

At present there are many anomalies in the system whereby

local education authorities allocate grants to students taking courses in higher or further education establishments.[15] Girls as well as boys may be deterred from taking courses because they cannot obtain any form of financial support whilst studying. At the present time many vocational and academic courses below degree level attract only discretionary grants, and these have often been early victims of cuts in educational spending. Athough in some areas students who attend college for only three days a week are allowed to draw social security payments at the same time (providing that they remain able to take up a job should a suitable vacancy occur), this is no real solution, as many courses of post-school study require attendance on more than three days a week. A report published in 1977 by the Manpower Services Commission suggests that 'work' should initially be abolished for the 16–19 age group, and that these years should be taken up with various forms of post-school training and work-experience schemes.[16] Although this might be helpful to many girls seeking post-school education, it still leaves unsolved the problems of mature women students and how their courses may be financed. The only practical solution would seem to be centrally-financed, mandatory grants for all students of any age-group taking full-time courses in further or higher education.

Mature students could, of course, also be helped in other ways. Some institutions of higher education already make provision for the admission of mature students to courses without formal entrance qualifications, but women often lack the confidence to apply for such courses; they could be encouraged to do so not only by the existence of financial security, but also by the existence of courses and facilities tailored to their needs. Mature students and younger students of both sexes, if they have the care of young children to consider, should be able to use child care facilities attached to the institutions at which they are studying, rather than having to search for alternative private and often very expensive sources of child care.

In some countries, for example in China and Sweden, policies of admission to courses of post-school education have placed emphasis on the equivalence of work experience to academic qualifications, although this has often proved to be

133

a cogent source of political controversy. In Sweden in July 1977 new admission plans for entry to post-school education were put into operation, giving equal currency to work experience, ability to complete the course, and formal educational qualifications.[17] The courses available to students in Swedish higher education also incorporate a high degree of flexibility, with points awarded for the completion of courses, and the possibility of taking courses part-time in the evenings, although this latter option does not usually apply in medicine, engineering or the natural sciences. Such plans may give women a greater chance of returning to study long after leaving school, but even in the Swedish system, the majority of those newly attracted into higher education appear to be opting initially for courses in administration, social work and cultural work professions, although more mature students are being attracted to medicine. Financial aid on a means-tested basis is available to all students taking courses in higher education, but often in the form of loans rather than grants. The number of female students in Swedish higher education has been increasing gradually since the mid-1960s, and for some years there have actually been more women than men students — the reverse of the situation in many industrial societies.[18] However, in technical courses men still predominate.[19]

The Swedish experience suggests two things of relevance to education in Britain. First, it indicates that more people — both men and women, and older people — are likely to gain access to higher education if that access is not entirely dependent on formal qualifications. Second, however, it is apparent that the tendency of women to specialize in the arts and social sciences is not necessarily overcome by a more open policy on admissions to higher education, although Sweden's male/female student ratio does destroy the belief that there will never be more women than men in higher education. The solution to the arts and social sciences specialization problem, however, clearly does not lie in higher education, but in the schools. What Britain should be careful to avoid is the kind of development which occurred in educational policy in Czechoslovakia in the 1960s, in an effort to halt the trend of feminization of particular disciplines in higher education and in certain occupations. There entry qualifications for boys to courses which were considered feminized were made considerably lower than the qualifications demanded for girls, with the result that many girls found themselves leaving school with no chance of a college place and few skills or prospects for employment.[20] If the tendency of women to specialize in the arts is to be reduced, it must surely be brought about in a positive rather than a negative way, with women being encouraged to take up science and technical subjects at school and after school, rather than simply being discouraged from studying arts subjects.

As with changes in schools, changes in further and higher education — given the decentralization of the British education system — may only be partially achieved by legislation, and much fighting may also have to be done by pressure groups. And it is important that men as well as women should be actively involved in these groups. For as Chafetz notes, men have so far avoided becoming collectively involved in the campaigns for the equality of women, even though some men as individuals may accept the legitimacy of the cause.[21] There are signs that some of the required changes will gradually come about, for example in relation to child care facilities and more flexible admissions policies, but if these are to be adopted in all post-school educational institutions, then pressure for changes to occur must not be decreased.

The Position of Women in Society — Present and Future

An important feature of the position of women as housewives in industrial societies is the isolated character of their labour and their partial or complete economic dependence on male breadwinners.[22] However, in Britain as in other societies, the extent of that isolation and economic dependence has begun to decline. Since the beginning of the 1950s there has been considerable growth in the proportion of the adult female population engaged in paid employment, and much of this increase has occurred amongst married women. At the same time the rate of marriage has been rising.[23] These two trends have given rise to a situation in which larger numbers of women than ever before have begun to sell their labour power for the greater portion of their lives, but also where

135

the degree of women's dependence on marriage has become more widespread than was previously the case.[24]

However, as most of the growth in female employment since 1960 has taken place amongst part-time workers[25] and because women's wages relative to men's still remain at two-thirds of the average male earnings,[26] it is difficult to understand Szymanski's argument that most working-class married women in capitalist societies are now economically independent of their husbands for much of their lives.[27] In fact, it would seem that in Britain only a few middle-class women acquire the kind of education and jobs which enable them to enjoy economic independence from men.[28] The majority of working-class women, despite their involvement in paid employment, continue to take primary responsibility for domestic labour and child care and remain at least partially economically dependent on men.[29] Amongst women who do work, union membership has been growing fast.[30] Although this is not necessarily indicative of women taking work more seriously, it does suggest that more women in employment are starting to regard matters of pay and work conditions as important rather than peripheral, and beginning to see reasonable wages and working conditions as a basic right to which women as well as men workers are entitled. But women often find it difficult to be active in their unions; branch meetings are frequently arranged after work hours, and in the evenings, when domestic commitments and care of children are likely to be at their most demanding.[31] And women trade unionists may find that when they take strike action, support from male trade unionists is limited. Other women may be reluctant to join unions, partly because they have been socialized into believing that their work is not amenable to unionism,[32] and partly because, in areas of employment such as shopwork, workers are isolated and easily victimized if they become union members.

The attitudes of women towards work and unions, as well as the continuing partial economic dependence of many women on men and the heavy involvement of women in domestic labour and child care, cannot be held to be solely the fault of the education that women receive. Certainly much of their education may convince women that their situation is either just or unchangeable, but education does

136

not create the subordination of women. It is indeed some-what disheartening to realize that the position of women in socialist societies is not markedly different from the position of women in most capitalist societies, despite some attempts to reduce the amount of sexism and sex-stereotyping found in the education offered to women in socialist societies.[33] In many socialist societies women are still found primarily in 'women's jobs' and do not have equal pay, although their jobs may include categories of employment such as engineer-ing, which are not considered 'women's jobs' in Britain.[34] Scott and Broyelle both note that in socialist societies women are no less likely than in capitalist societies to be involved in domestic labour and child care to such an extent that any other activities, whether paid employment, politi-cal activity or leisure interests, take second place.[35]

Does this then mean that the position of women is un-changeable whether under a capitalist or socialist mode of production, so that no matter what changes are made in the educational opportunities and consciousness of women or in society nothing fundamental is altered? Certainly, those who have analysed the position of women in socialist societies do not accept this. For example, Scott points out that both Marx and Engels assumed that the family in capitalist socie-ties was a function of private property, and that the family would disappear with the abolition of private property, taking with it the subordinate position of women. This belief, Scott suggests, had detracted attention from the real barriers to women's equal development, which she sees as the domi-nance of patriarchical beliefs, the fact that women work out-side the home in jobs and work environments which have been structured by men for their own convenience, and the continued existence of a dual role for women.[36] Scott says (1976, p. 190): 'as long as a woman is regarded as having two roles while a man has only one, women and men will never find themselves on equal footing'. Effectively this argument claims that better educational and job opportunities for women are insufficient to bring about a change in their posi-tion. It is of no use women being taught the sciences and technical subjects, and men being trained in domestic skills, if those skills are not utilized once individuals leave school. Just as it is possible for a woman who has received a scientific

137

education to enter a traditionally 'feminine' job afterwards, or to treat a job as less important than a man would, so it is perfectly possible for a man who knows how to cook, wash, clean and care for children never to offer to do any of these things. The connections between knowledge and action are rarely as close as either reformers or revolutionaries sometimes think they are.

What is needed then, to change the position of women in both socialist and capitalist societies, is a closer link between knowledge and action. The transition to socialism has not brought with it the liberation of women, or men, from the sexual division of labour:[37]

> The abolition of private ownership of the means of production does not bring about the end of the single family as the economic unit of society nor the transformation of private housekeeping into a social industry. Even when the best intentions are present, there must also be an economic base sufficiently strong and well-organised to assume these economic functions. At the same time there must be a theoretical concept and a plan of action. So far no socialist society has met these conditions.

The replacement of the family by alternative forms of collective or communal living is not necessarily a solution to the freeing of women from their dual roles. In Israel the kibbutzim have not altogether succeeded in ending the sexual division of labour, nor have they been completely successful in breaking down the boundaries of conventional kin and family life. As Tiger and Shepher note (1977, p. 92):

> The sex typing of labour is obvious. Agriculture, industry, construction and auxiliary shops . . . management, economic and political activity, and movement or outside work are predominantly male. Service, consumption and education are predominantly female.

The same authors also comment on the growing importance of family life in many Kibbutzim since their formation (1977, p. 210):

> With the birth of children, the family gradually achieved wider legitimacy. This became easier as new groups joined

the kibbutzim. Nevertheless, until the War of Liberation, the family as an institution remained modest and inconspicuous. After the war, the family became more visible and began to acquire broader functions, especially in consumption and education.

However, the Kibbutz has demonstrated that not all of the tasks traditionally performed by the family need necessarily be carried out individually rather than collectively, for instance washing, cooking and cleaning. Certainly it would be possible, without altering the family unit at all, to transfer some of the domestic labour presently undertaken within it to outside service institutions such as laundries and restaurants. In certain of its housing and planning projects, Sweden has gone some way towards the achievement of such socialization of housework tasks outside the home, maintaining the family unit, but at the same time breaking down its isolation from other people.[38]

Child care, of course, remains a central problem in relation to the family and the position of women, and here the Israeli Kibbutzim have vascillated between caring for all children in communal nurseries, and expecting much of the work of child care to be carried out by individual parents. In many socialist societies a controversy rages over whether child care is best solved by nursery provision outside the home, or whether the answer is perhaps to offer paid leave from employment to either men or women, so that both sexes have the opportunity to become active parents and to work outside the home.[39] The difficulty with the second solution is that unless men are brought up to think that child care is part of their adult responsibilities, women will continue to be the ones who give up work to rear children. Whichever solution is adopted, child care is an issue which must be taken up and dealt with by the state.

Broyelle argues that the socialization of housework and child care is in any case insufficient to alter the position of women. She suggests that a further change in the organization and definition of work is also necessary. This is the abolition of the distinction between manual labour and intellectual work, a distinction which effectively prevents the equal participation of women in production because it is often argued that women cannot undertake heavy manual work, and therefore do not deserve an equal place in society alongside men. If manual and intellectual work were less separated into different kinds of jobs, and if gender characteristics were no longer attached to these types of work (and to the evaluation of their worth), then both men and women might stand to gain.[40] As Willis has shown for education, the division between manual and mental activity causes a significant gulf between the cultural worlds of working-class boys and girls.[41] If this cultural gulf could be bridged, then the basis of sex-stereotyping would be significantly reduced. But this is a change which cannot be legislated and planned for. Educational policies and practices would thus be invaluable as a way of changing people's attitudes towards manual and mental activities.

Do Women want Change?

It may be that the kinds of change in the education of women and in the organization of society which have been suggested here will be seen as idealistic or as unrealistic by some women. Other women may argue that they would prefer to retain their traditional roles within the family and the sexual division of labour, that they are better off as they are. Any social change is likely to be perceived by at least some of the individuals affected by it as threatening and undesirable, and the prospects of a change in the position of women may well be frightening to those women who feel secure in their role as housewives and mothers. There is, of course, no question of compelling people to change either their ideas or their behaviour. Women have a choice; to stay as they are, or to try to alter that position so that they have greater equality with men. The first choice they possess as individuals, the second they will only achieve collectively. Analysis of women in capitalist and socialist societies suggests that many of them are not happy with the *status quo*, and that they are trying to bring about changes. In many countries in the world now women are fighting for the right to greater participation in economic, political and social affairs; for the socialization of housework and child care; and for the right to be recognized as people rather than as sex objects, possessions or inferior beings. The choice of women then, is beginning to be made. It is more likely to be an informed and successful choice if both women and men come to be educated in a non-sexist way. The achievement of an education for both women and men which does not falsely and artificially limit thought, skills and abilities on the basis of gender will not be easy in any society, but not to attempt something because it will be difficult is a coward's way out. A non-sexist education is part of a much more complex struggle for the liberation of women; but it is a part of that struggle which must have a high priority, for action without knowledge is no better than knowledge without action. And women must not only educate and persuade other women to fight for changes, whether these are legislative, organizational or attitudinal, they must also educate and persuade men that changes are necessary, not just in education but in the whole organization of society. The arguments in favour of a non-sexist system of education are a good point at which to commence this persuasion; there is no other way in which the full creative and flexible potential of human beings, so essential to the liberation of people, will begin to be realized.

Notes

Chapter I The Entry of Women into Mass Education in a Capitalist Society

1   See Lawson and Silver, 1973; Lowndes, 1969; Sturt, 1967.
2   See for instance Williams, 1965; Douglas, 1967; Floud, Halsey and Anderson, 1961.
3   Referred to by Marks, 1976.
4   These have included: Committee of the Secondary Schools Examination Council, 1943; Central Advisory Council for Education, 1959; Central Advisory Council for Education, 1963; Committee on Higher Education, 1963; Central Advisory Council for Education, 1967.
5   The Women's Liberation Movement should not be seen as a tightly organized body; it is a loose collection of groups of women dedicated to furthering feminism and the liberation of women in any or all of various aspects of life — education, sex, work, social life etc. Although people often talk of 'the Women's Movement thinking x' or 'believing y', there are many shades of opinion involved between and within different groups.
6   The main pieces of legislation passed in Great Britain which relate to the equal treatment of men and women are the 1970 Equal Pay Act and the 1975 Sex Discrimination Act. For further details of these and their achievements, see Coussins, 1976.
7   See for instance work on the schooling of women in Sharpe, 1976; Marks, 1976; Blackstone, 1976; Turner, 1974.
8   The importance of these two institutions, the family and the school, to the maintenance of the existing structure of capitalist societies is discussed by Althusser, 1971; Bourdieu, 1973; Benton, 1974.

142

9 See Barker and Allen, 1976a and 1976b.
10 See Mitchell, 1971; also see discussion of the role of the family in capitalist society in Secombe, 1974; Gardiner, 1975.
11 Althusser, 1971.
12 Ibid., pp. 138-9.
13 Poulantzas, 1975.
14 Bourdieu, 1973.
15 Althusser, 1971.
16 See Kamm, 1965; Turner, 1974; Sturt, 1967.
17 See Sharpe, 1976, and Wolpe, 1977.
18 Kamm, 1965; Turner, 1974.
19 Williams, 1965, gives an account of the different groups involved in the nineteenth-century expansion of education to the masses.
20 Look for instance at Alexander, 1976; Thompson, 1976; Davies, 1975.
21 The first Factory Act which affected women was not until the 1840s. Women were stopped from underground work in 1842, but their conditions of employment in factories were not regulated until after 1844.
22 See Best, 1971. He estimates a total of 1,200,000 female domestic servants in 1861.
23 See Dale, 1974 and DES Education Survey 21, 1975.
24 Parry and Parry, 1974.
25 See Sturt, 1967.
26 Turner, 1974.
27 Aries, 1975.
28 Evidence from A. Davin, quoted by Sharpe, 1976.
29 Sharpe, 1976.
30 See Marks, 1976.
31 Quoted from the Bryce Commission by Lawson and Silver, 1973, p. 343.
32 See Sharpe, 1976; Blackstone, 1976; Mackie and Patullo, 1977; Barron and Norris, 1976.
33 See Adams, 1975.
34 Coussins, 1976 gives an account of the early progress of the Sex Discrimination Act.
35 See Banks, 1954, for an assessment of middle-class family planning in the Victorian era.
36 Laslett, 1965.
37 Committee of the Secondary Schools Examination Council, 1943.
38 Sharpe, 1976, Chapter I.
39 See DES Education Survey 21, 1975.

Chapter 2 Sexism, Socialization and Culture in the Education of Girls

1 Althusser, 1971.
2 For example see Williams, 1965; Bourdieu, 1973; Stenhouse, 1967; Young, 1971.
3 Williams, 1965.
4 See Midwinter, 1972; Keddie, 1974; Bernstein, 1972; Bourdieu, 1973.
5 Midwinter, 1972; Keddie, 1974; Bourdieu, 1973; Bernstein, 1972.
6 See Bourdieu, 1973 and Bernstein, 1975.
7 See Jackson, 1962; Lunn, 1970; Bernstein, 1971; Sharpe, 1976; DES Education Survey 21, 1975.
8 Stenhouse, 1967.
9 Bourdieu, 1973.
10 For instance the women featured in Rapoport and Rapoport, 1976.
11 Chafetz, 1974.
12 Samuel, 1976.
13 Adams and Laurikietis, 1976.
14 Wolpe, 1977.
15 Ibid., pp. 36–8.
16 For example see Tiger and Shepher, 1977.
17 For instance, a description of 'changing sex' is given by Morris, 1975.
18 See Weitz, 1977.
19 Anthropological studies which deal with cultural variations in the position of women may be found in Rosaldo and Lamphere, 1974; Mead, 1962; Reiter, 1975.
20 Thompson, 1903, summarized by Klein, 1946.
21 Summarized in Klein, 1946.
22 Terman and Miles, summarized in Klein, 1946.
23 Maccoby, 1966; see also Maccoby, 1972.
24 Maccoby, 1966.
25 Douglas, 1967.
26 Douglas *et al.*, 1968; and Maccoby, 1966 and 1972.
27 Douglas, 1967.
28 Ibid., also Maccoby, 1966 and 1972.
29 Maccoby, 1966 and 1972.
30 Ibid.
31 Hudson, 1966.
32 Maccoby, 1972.
33 Ibid., also Maccoby, 1966.
34 Maccoby, 1972.
35 Fogelman, 1969–70.

36 Douglas, 1967. See also Brierley, 1975.
37 Banks, 1976.
38 Douglas *et al.*, 1968.
39 Douglas, 1967, p. 103.
40 Ibid.
41 Dale, 1974.
42 Douglas *et al.*, 1968.
43 DES Statistics of Education, vol. 2, 1976.
44 Ibid.
45 Ibid.
46 DES Education Survey 21, 1975.
47 Chafetz, 1974.
48 Goldberg and Lewis, 1972.
49 Newson and Newson, 1963.
50 Kohlberg, 1966.
51 Newson and Newson, 1963.
52 For example see Chafetz, 1974; Maccoby, 1966; Belotti, 1975.
53 Newson and Newson, 1976.
54 Goldberg and Lewis, 1972.
55 Ibid.
56 Newson and Newson, 1976.
57 Ibid.
58 Ibid., Chapter 4. See also Belotti, 1975, p. 84.
59 Newson and Newson, 1976.
60 Belotti, 1975, Chapter I.
61 Newson and Newson, 1976.
62 Ibid.
63 Ibid.
64 Ibid.
65 Ibid., p. 325.
66 Ibid., p. 378.
67 Althusser, 1971.
68 McRobbie and Garber, 1976.
69 Ibid. See also McRobbie, 1977.
70 See Smith, 1973.
71 The blurring of work and leisure in the lives of women is dealt with by Oakley, 1976.
72 McRobbie and Garber, 1976.
73 Ibid.
74 McRobbie, 1977.
75 Ibid.
76 Llewellyn, 1977.
77 Ibid.
78 Sharpe, 1976.
79 Ibid. See also Knight, 1977, and Branston, 1977.

80 Branston, 1977.
81 Research on classroom interaction may be found in Woods and Hammersley, 1977 and Hammersley and Woods, 1976.
82 But see Delamont, 1976.
83 Furlong, 1977 and 1976.
84 See Chapter 4.
85 Lambert, 1976.
86 Delamont, 1976, p. 69.
87 Ibid., p. 71.
88 Dale, 1969 and 1971.
89 Frazier and Sadker, 1973.
90 Wolpe, 1977.
91 Delamont, 1976, quoted from Moody, 1968.
92 As used by Kerr, 1968 and 1971.
93 Bourdieu, 1973.
94 For details of some of these see Fairbairns, 1975.
95 See DES education Survey 21, 1975.
96 Ibid. See also Sharpe, 1976.
97 Dale, 1974.
98 DES Education Survey 21, 1975.
99 Ibid.
100 Dale, 1974.
101 DES Education Survey 21, 1975.
102 Sharpe, 1976.
103 See observation of lesson by Keddie, 1971; see also Sharpe, 1976, p. 150.
104 Griffiths, 1977.
105 Mentioned by Davies, 1976.
106 Quoted by Adams and Laurikietis, 1976, p. 29.
107 Central Advisory Council for Education, 1967.
108 See Bennett, 1976.
109 Sexism in children's literature is dealt with by Belotti, 1975; Frazier and Sadker, 1973; Children's Rights Workshop, 1976.
110 Adams and Laurikietis, 1976.
111 Ibid.
112 DES Statistics of Education, vol. 4, 1974.
113 See Belotti, 1975, for a discussion about the teaching of young children as a 'feminine' role.
114 See Deem, 1973.
115 Sharpe, 1976, pp. 145-6.
116 Quoted by Dale, 1969, p. 100.
117 Ibid.
118 Wolpe, 1977, pp. 35-6.
119 Ibid., p. 36.
120 Harrison, 1974.

121 Frazier and Sadker, 1973.
122 Douglas, 1967; Griffiths, 1977.
123 Llewellyn, 1977.
124 Sharpe, 1976, Ch. 5.
125 Hussain, 1976.
126 Quoted from *Times Educational Supplement* by *Women and Education* newsletter, no. 11, p. 7.
127 See Hussain, 1976; Bowles and Gintis, 1976; Althusser, 1971.
128 Barron and Norris, 1976.

Chapter 3 Patterns of Contemporary Curricular Discrimination and Differentiation in the Education of Girls

1 See Rubenstein and Simon, 1969; also Fenwick, 1976.
2 For example, Central Advisory Council for Education, 1959; Central Advisory Council for Education, 1963; Committee on Higher Education, 1963; Central Advisory Council for Education, 1967.
3 Details of these can be found in DES, 1977. See also Hextall, 1977.
4 Banks, 1955.
5 See Silver, 1973.
6 Finn and Grant, 1977.
7 Ibid., see also Fenwick, 1976.
8 See Banks, 1976; Bernstein, 1971; Newson and Newson, 1968.
9 As noted in the Gurney-Dixon Report, 1954.
10 Committee of the Secondary Schools Examination Council, 1943.
11 Central Advisory Council for Education, 1959.
12 Central Advisory Council for Education, 1963.
13 Committee on Higher Education, 1963.
14 Central Advisory Council for Education, 1967.
15 Douglas, 1967.
16 Figures from *Times Educational Supplement*, 21 March 1975.
17 Quoted by Fenwick, 1976, p. 128.
18 Benn and Simon, 1970.
19 DES Education Survey 21, 1975.
20 Ibid.
21 Ibid.
22 DES Statistics of Education, vol. 2, 1974.
23 Barker, 1977.
24 Gibb, 1977.
25 As reported in the *Times Educational Supplement*, 1 July 1977, p. 9.
26 Notably Dale, 1969, 1971 and 1974.

27 Dale, 1974.
28 Ibid.; see also Dale, 1969 and 1971.
29 Dale, 1969.
30 Dale, 1974.
31 Ormerod, 1975; Atherton, 1972–3; Campbell, 1969.
32 Miller and Dale, 1974.
33 Dale, 1971.
34 Blackstone, 1976.
35 Young, 1971; Finn and Grant, 1977.
36 For example, these include Cox and Dyson, 1971; Boyson and Cox, 1977; also, Bennett, 1976.
37 See Deem, 1973.
38 Hencke, 1976.
39 See Fairhall, 1977a.
40 DES, 1976.
41 DES, 1977.
42 Coussins, 1976.
43 Byrne, 1976.
44 See Coussins, 1976, and *Women and Education* newsletter, no. 10, 1977, pp. 10–11.
45 Byrne, 1977.

Chapter 4 Women in Higher Education

1 See for example, Caine, 1969; Borer, 1976; Turner, 1974; Kamm, 1965; Sturt, 1967.
 2 The position of women in contemporary societies is examined in a number of papers to be found in Barker and Allen, 1976a and 1976b.
 3 See Davies, 1975.
 4 In 1976, 36.4 per cent of students entering universities in Britain were female; numbers of women students entering British polytechnics in this year were also higher than in previous years.
 5 Notably in the Committee on Higher Education, 1963.
 6 For example, see reports of speeches made by Shirley Williams, Secretary of State for Education and Science in 1977, about policy on higher education; Fairhall, 1977b; Hencke, 1977b.
 7 The Committee on Higher Education Report, 1963.
 8 See Davies, 1975.
 9 Taylor, 1965.
10 Borer, 1976, p. 254.
11 Tropp, 1957.

12 Floud and Scott, 1961.
13 Far more girls than boys enter teacher training; for example in 1973–4 3,070 boys and 13,170 girls of that year's school leavers took up places on courses of initial teacher training. See DES *Statistics of Education*, vol. 2, 1974, Table 1, p. 11. Although colleges of education have begun to diversify their courses, these will not necessarily replace teacher-training courses as a form of higher education for girls, particularly if they require two 'A' levels. In 1976 only 49.2 per cent of women entering teacher training had two or more 'A' levels. See *Times Educational Supplement*, 19 August 1977, p. 4.
14 The Committee on Higher Education, 1963.
15 See Burgess and Pratt, 1970, for an account of the transition from CATs to universities.
16 Donaldson, 1975.
17 See *Times Educational Supplement*, 4 August 1977, p. 4.
18 See Blackstone and Fulton, 1975.
19 Ibid., p. 270.
20 McIntosh, 1975.
21 Ibid.
22 See *Guardian*, 1977a.
23 *Times Educational Supplement*, 4 February 1977, p. 4.
24 For figures relating to sociology, see British Sociological Association Working Party, 1975.
25 For example, see Webb, 1975 and Webb, 1977.
26 Blackstone and Fulton, 1975.
27 See *Guardian*, 1977b.
28 See Hencke, 1977b.
29 McDonald, 1976.
30 See Byrne, 1975.
31 Data on this may be found in Williams *et al.*, 1974.
32 For instance, women applicants to medical schools prior to the passing of the Sex Discrimination Act in 1975, were subject to an admissions quota, regardless of 'A' level grades. See Blackstone and Fulton, 1975.
33 Research on what influences student choice of higher education courses suggests that males are more likely than females to have selected their 'A' level subjects in relation to a particular career or higher education course. See McCreath, 1970.
34 See Deem, 1976a.
35 Harris, 1970, p. 285.
36 Smith, 1976.
37 See Deem, 1976a.
38 Webb, 1977.
39 Frazier and Sadker, 1973.

40 Womens Studies courses have expanded enormously in recent years especially in further and higher education. See Fairbairns, 1974.
41 Bernstein, 1971.
42 Bowles and Gintis, 1976, p. 11.
43 See McIntosh, 1975. Figures for UCCA in 1971 of successful female university applicants in biology, botany and zoology, 44 per cent; in physics, 13 per cent.
44 Stéhelin, 1976, p. 78.
45 Sharpe, 1976, Chapters 4 and 5.
46 See Althusser, 1971.
47 Webb, 1977; Deem, 1976; Friedan, 1963; Harris, 1970; Graham, 1973.
48 Webb, 1977; Deem, 1976a.
49 Webb, 1977.
50 Frazier and Sadker, 1973.
51 For example, a female friend of the author's with a first class honours degree was once told by a careers adviser that for her to find employment would be much more difficult than if she were 'a weedy male with a third class degree'.
52 Some of the problems faced by women doctoral students are currently being examined by Daphne Taylorson in research for a doctoral dissertation in the Department of Sociology, University of Manchester.
53 Webb, 1977. For example in sociology, Webb argues, women are often interested in the applications of sociology to practical fields, whilst men may prefer theoretical sociology. Within the discipline, higher academic status is attached to the latter.
54 For example, see *Guardian*, 1977b and 1977c.
55 See Coussins, 1976.
56 Blackstone and Fulton, 1975.
57 Ibid. See also Halmos, 1970.
58 Blackstone and Fulton, 1975.
59 Ibid.
60 Ibid.
61 See Moodie and Eustace, 1974; Donaldson, 1975; Burgess and Pratt, 1974.
62 Moodie and Eustace, 1974.
63 Edwards, 1976.
64 See Smith, 1976, for a discussion of a similar analysis in relation to women journalists.
65 Whitehead, 1976.
66 As already successfully operated by the Open University admissions scheme.

Chapter 5 Women as Teachers – Separate and Unequal?

1 See Simpson and Simpson, 1969; Leggatt, 1970; Kelsall and Kelsall, 1969.
2 Tropp, 1957, looks at the early struggles of elementary teachers to control or improve their conditions and status.
3 Floud and Scott, 1961.
4 Simpson and Simpson, 1969; Zeigler, 1967.
5 Deem, 1973; see also Deem, 1976b.
6 For example, as in Althusser, 1971; Bourdieu, 1973; Poulantzas, 1975; David, 1977.
7 David, 1977.
8 Gibson, 1970-1.
9 See Deem, 1976b and Gosden, 1972.
10 This point is made by Hoyle, 1969.
11 Cortis, 1972-3.
12 See Deem, 1973.
13 Parry and Parry, 1974.
14 Bowles and Gintis, 1976.
15 Musgrove, 1971.
16 Richardson, 1973.
17 DES Statistics of Education, 1974, vol. 4, p. 25.
18 Central Advisory Council for Education, 1967, p. 332.
19 DES Statistics of Education, 1974, vol. 1.
20 Norris, 1977, pp. 3-4.
21 As for example by Leggatt, 1970; Simpson and Simpson, 1969; Hoyle, 1969; Grace, 1972.
22 Central Advisory Council for Education, 1967.
23 Pollard, 1974, p. 75.
24 A study of married women teachers has been carried out by Shepherd, 1970-1.
25 Hellawell and Smithers, 1973-4.
26 Grace, 1972.
27 See study of teachers' reasons for choice of work areas, Halmos, 1970.
28 See discussion of this point in Parry and Parry, 1974.
29 Dealt with by Tropp, 1957. See also Taylor, 1969.
30 Parry and Parry, 1974.
31 Considered in an analysis of teacher training by Kamm, 1965, Chapter 19.
32 Ibid., p. 275. See also Taylor, 1969.
33 Kamm, 1965, p. 278 and also Taylor, 1969.
34 DES Committee of Enquiry, 1972.
35 DES, 1977.

36 Bennett, 1976.
37 Ibid., p. 55.
38 Hannam, Smith and Stephenson, 1976.
39 Ibid., pp. 84-6.
40 Dale, 1969, pp. 89-115.
41 See Deem, 1976b and Coates, 1972.
42 The implications of this are discussed by Roy, 1968 and Manzer, 1970.
43 See Deem, 1976b.
44 Zeigler, 1967.
45 For instance, see Bain, 1970.
46 See Deem, 1973 and Coates, 1972.
47 See Deem, 1973.
48 Ibid., pp. 103-30.
49 Deem, 1976b.
50 The relative chances of promotion for different categories of teachers were worked out by Manzer, 1970.

Chapter 6 Women, Education and Society: the Possibilities of Change

1 Sexism in children's books is discussed in detail in Children's Rights Workshop, 1976.
2 This dependence was argued to exist by Ivor Wymer, Prospective Labour Parliamentary candidate for Ludlow, in a talk 'Careers and further education', at Shrewsbury Labour Club, 5 November 1977. See also Hencke, 1977c.
3 Figures and an analysis of the role of the Job Creation Scheme in relation to girl school leavers are to be found in Scott, 1977.
4 See Mackie, 1977.
5 Ibid.
6 DES, 1976, p. 3.
7 Ibid., p. 4.
8 For example, see Fairhall, 1977c.
9 As suggested by a senior chief-inspector of the DES in 1977. See *Guardian*, 1977c.
10 See DES Education Survey 21, 1975.
11 Willis, 1977.
12 *Times Higher Education Supplement*, 1977.
13 Ibid.
14 See McIntosh, 1975.
15 See Judd, 1977.
16 Hencke, 1977c.

17 Details from Sandgren, 1977.
18 Ibid., pp. 24–5.
19 Ibid.
20 Scott, 1976.
21 Chafetz, 1974, p. 231.
22 See Gardiner, 1976.
23 Davies, 1975.
24 See Gardiner, 1977.
25 Ibid.
26 Davies, 1975.
27 Szymanski, 1976.
28 See Gardiner, 1977.
29 Ibid.
30 In 1972 the number of unionized women increased by 5.4 per cent, compared with a growth rate for unionized men of only 0.7 per cent. But the number of women not in unions is also rising. See Davies, 1975, pp. 151–3.
31 Karpf, 1977.
32 Ibid. Reporting on a conference of women from public-sector unions, Karpf notes the comments of a nurse who said that unionism was often felt to be antithetical to good nursing.
33 Information about the position of women in socialist societies may be found in Broyelle, 1977; Scott, 1976; Davin, 1976; Rowbotham, 1972.
34 Ibid.
35 Scott, 1976 and Broyelle, 1977.
36 Scott, 1976.
37 Ibid., p. 208.
38 Scott, 1976.
39 Ibid. Also Broyelle, 1977.
40 Broyelle, 1977.
41 Willis, 1977.

Bibliography

Adams, C. and Laurikietis, K. (1976), *The Gender Trap*, vol. 2, Virago, London.

Adams, R. (1975), *A Woman's Place*, Chatto and Windus, London.

Alexander, S. (1976), 'Women's work in nineteenth century London', in J. Mitchell and A. Oakley, *The Rights and Wrongs of Women*, Penguin, Harmondsworth.

Althusser, L. (1971), 'Ideology and Ideological State Apparatuses', in *Lenin and Philosophy and other Essays*, New Left Books, London.

Anderson, S. (1972), *Sex Differences and Discrimination in Education*, Wadsworth, California.

Aries, P. (1975), *Centuries of Childhood*, Penguin, Harmondsworth.

Atherton, B. F. (1972-3), 'Co-educational and single-sex schooling and happiness of marriage', *Educational Research*, vol. 15, pp. 221-6.

Bain, G. S. (1970), *The Growth of White-Collar Unionism*, Clarendon Press, Oxford.

Banks, J. A. (1954), *Prosperity and Parenthood*, Routledge & Kegan Paul, London.

Banks, O. (1955), *Parity and Prestige in English Secondary Education*, Routledge & Kegan Paul, London.

Banks, O. (1976), *The Sociology of Education*, Batsford, London.

Bardwick, J. M. (1972), *Readings on the Psychology of Women*, Harper & Row, New York.

Barker, D. L. (1977), 'Opportunities and choice in the curriculum', unpublished paper given to 'Teaching Girls to be Women' Conference, University of Essex, 30 April.

Barker, D. L. and Allen, S. (1976a), *Dependence and Exploitation in Work and Marriage*, Longmans, London.

Barker, D. L. and Allen, S. (1976b), *Sexual Divisions and Society: Process and Change*, Tavistock, London, 1976.

Barron, R. D. and Norris, G. M. (1976), 'Sexual divisions and the dual labour market', in Barker and Allen, 1976b.

Belotti, E. (1975), *Little Girls*, Writers and Readers Publishing Co-operative, London.

Benn, C. and Simon, B. (1970), *Half Way There*, McGraw Hill, Maidenhead.

Bennett, N. (1976), *Teaching Style and Pupil Progress*, Open Books, London.

Benton, T. (1974), 'Education and Politics', in D. Holly, *Education or Domination*, Arrow, London.

Bernstein, B. (1971), 'On the classification and framing of knowledge', in M. F. D. Young, *Knowledge and Control*, Macmillan, London.

Bernstein, B. (1972), *Class, Codes and Control*, vol. 1, Routledge & Kegan Paul, London.

Bernstein, B. (1975), *Class, Codes and Control*, vol. 3, Routledge & Kegan Paul, London.

Best, G. (1971),*Mid-Victorian Britain*, Weidenfeld & Nicolson, London.

Blackstone, T. (1976), 'The education of girls today', in J. Mitchell and A. Oakley, *The Rights and Wrongs of Women*, Penguin, Harmondsworth.

Blackstone, T. and Fulton, O. (1975), 'Sex discrimination among university teachers: a British–American comparison', *British Journal of Sociology*, vol. 26, September, pp. 261-75.

Borer, M. (1976), *Willingly to School*, Lutterworth Press, London.

Bourdieu, P. (1973), 'Cultural reproduction and social reproduction', in R. Brown, *Knowledge, Education and Cultural Change*, Tavistock, London.

Bowles, S. and Gintis, H. (1976), *Schooling in Capitalist America*, Routledge & Kegan Paul, London.

Boyson, R. and Cox, C. B. (1977), *Black Paper*, Maurice Temple Smith, London.

Branston, F. (1977), 'Asian girls; how they integrate; how they don't', *Cosmopolitan*, June, pp. 84-94.

Brierley, J. (1975), 'Sex differences in education', *Trends in Education*, February, pp. 17-24.

British Sociological Association, Working Party (1975), 'Report on status of women in the profession', 13 Endsleigh Street, London, WC1.

Broyelle, C. (1977), *Women's Liberation in China*, Harvester Press, London.

Burgess, T. and Pratt, J. (1970), *Policy and Practice: Colleges of Advanced Technology*, Allen Lane, London.

Burgess, T. and Pratt, J. (1974), *Polytechnics: a Report*, Pitman, London.

Byrne, E. (1975), 'The place of women in the changing pattern of higher education', London University Teaching Methods Unit Conference proceedings, *Women in Higher Education*, London, pp. 1–9.

Byrne, E. (1976), report of meeting with Women and Education group and National Council for Civil Liberties, *Women and Education*, no. 9, p. 3, Manchester.

Byrne, E. (1977), interview in *Women and Education*, no. 10, p. 11, Manchester.

Caine, S. (1969), *British Universities: Purpose and Prospect*, Bodley Head, London.

Campbell, R. J. (1969), 'Co-education: attitudes and self-concepts of girls at three schools', *British Journal of Educational Psychology*, vol. 39, p. 87.

Central Advisory Council for Education (1959), *15–18*, HMSO (Crowther Report).

Central Advisory Council for Education (1963), *Half our Future*, HMSO (Newsom Report).

Central Advisory Council for Education (1967), *Children and their Primary Schools*, HMSO (Plowden Report).

Chafetz, J. S. (1974), *Masculine/Feminine or Human?*, F. R. Peacock, Illinois.

Children's Rights Workshop (1976), *Sexism in Children's Books*, Writers and Readers Publishing Co-operative, London.

Coates, R. D. (1972), *Teachers Unions and Interest-group Politics*, Cambridge University Press.

Committee of the Secondary Schools Examination Council (1943), *Curriculum and Examinations in Secondary Schools*, HMSO (Norwood Report).

Committee on Higher Education (1963), *Higher Education*, HMSO (Robbins Report).

Cortis, G. A. (1972–3), 'An analysis of some differences between primary and secondary teachers', *Educational Research*, vol. 15, pp. 109–14.

Coussins, J. (1976), *The Equality Report*, National Council for Civil Liberties, London.

Cox, C. B. and Dyson, A. E. (1971), *The Black Papers on Education*, Davis Poynter, London.

Dale, R. R. (1969), *Mixed or Single Sex School*, vol. 1, Routledge & Kegan Paul, London.

Dale, R. R. (1971), *Mixed or Single-Sex School: Some social aspects*, vol. 2, Routledge & Kegan Paul, London.

Dale, R. R. (1974), *Mixed or Single-Sex School: Attainment, attitudes and over-view*, vol. 3, Routledge & Kegan Paul, London.

David, M. (1977), 'The State, education and the family', paper read to British Sociological Association Conference 'Power and the State', University of Sheffield, April.

Davies, L. (1976), 'Schooling and sex roles', paper read to BSA Midlands Women's Caucus meeting, University of Leicester, February.

Davies, R. (1975), *Women and Work*, Arrow, London.

Davin, A. (1976), *Childhood*, vol. 2, History Workshop series, quoted by Sharpe, S. (1976), *Just Like a Girl*, Penguin, Harmondsworth.

Davin, D. (1976), *Woman-Work*, Clarendon Press, Oxford.

Deem, R. (1973), 'A sociological analysis of the relationship between militancy and professionalism amongst secondary school teachers in England and Wales', unpublished M.Phil., University of Leicester.

Deem, R. (1976a), 'Women, curricula and authority in higher education', paper read to BSA Midlands Women's Caucus, University of Nottingham.

Deem, R. (1976b), 'Professionalism, unity and militant action; the case of teachers', *Sociological Review*, vol. 24, no. 1, February, pp. 43-61.

Delamont, S. (1976), *Interaction in the Classroom*, Methuen, London.

Department of Education and Science (DES) (1975), *Curricular Differences for Boys and Girls*, Education Survey 21, HMSO.

DES Committee of Enquiry (1972), *Teacher Education and Training*, HMSO (James Report).

DES (1976), *Educating our Children: Four Subjects for Debate*, DES.

DES (1977), *Education in Schools: A Consultative Document*, HMSO (Green Paper).

DES Statistics of Education 1974, vol. 1, *Schools*, HMSO, 1975.

DES Statistics of Education 1974, vol. 2, *School Leavers*, HMSO, 1976.

DES Statistics of Education 1974, vol. 3, *Further Education*, HMSO, 1974.

DES Statistics of Education 1974, vol. 4, *Teachers*, HMSO, 1974.

Donaldson, L. (1975), *Policy and the Polytechnics*, Saxon House, London.

Douglas, J. W. B. (1967), *The Home and the School*, Panther, London.

Douglas, J. W. B. *et al.* (1968), *All Our Future*, Peter Davies, London.

Edwards, E. G. (1976), 'Power and authority in the university; power and purpose', Society for Research into Higher Education Conference, Proceedings, University of Surrey, Guildford.

Fairbairns, Z. (1975), *Women's Studies in the UK*, London Seminars.

Fairhall, J. (1977a), 'Schools council told to reform', *Guardian*, 20 January.

Fairhall, J. (1977b), 'Girls spurn engineer's apprenticeship offer', *Guardian*, 25 February.

Fairhall, J. (1977c) 'DES plotting sinister takeover', *Guardian*, 13 April.

Fenwick, R. G. (1976), *The Comprehensive School, 1944-70*, Methuen, London.

Finn, D. and Grant, N. (1977), 'Social democracy and the educational crisis', paper read to BSA study group, University of Leicester, February.

Bibliography

Floud, J., Halsey, A. H. and Anderson, C. A. (1961), *Education, Economy and Society*, Free Press, New York.

Floud, J. and Scott, W. (1961), 'Recruitment to teaching in England and Wales', in Floud, Halsey and Anderson (1961).

Fogelman, K. R. (1969-70), 'Piagetian tests and sex differences', *Educational Research*, vol. 12, pp. 154-5.

Frazier, N. and Sadker, M. (1973), *Sexism in School and Society*, Harper & Row, New York.

Friedan, B. (1963), *The Feminine Mystique*, Norton, New York.

Furlong, V. (1976), 'Interaction sets in the classroom', in M. Hammersley and P. Woods, *The Process of Schooling*, Routledge & Kegan Paul, 1977.

Furlong, V. (1977), 'Anancy goes to school', in M. Hammersley and P. Woods, *School Experience*, Croom-Helm, London.

Gardiner, J. (1975), 'The role of domestic labour', *New Left Review*, no. 89, January-February, pp. 47-58.

Gardiner, J. (1976), 'Political economy of domestic labour in capitalist society', in Barker and Allen (1976a).

Gardiner, J. (1977), 'Women in the labour process and class structure', paper read to BSA Sexual Divisions Study group, University of Sheffield, April.

Gibb, F. (1977), 'Working women are still less equal', *Times Higher Education Supplement*, 30 September 1977, p. 2.

Gibson, R. (1970-1), 'The role of the primary and secondary school teacher', *Educational Research*, vol. 13, pp. 20-7.

Goldberg, S. and Lewis, M. (1972), 'Play behaviour in the year old infant: early sex differences', in Bardwick (1972).

Gosden, P. J. H. (1972), *The Evolution of a Profession*, Basil Blackwell, Oxford.

Grace, G. R. (1972), *Role Conflict and the Teacher*, Routledge & Kegan Paul, London.

Graham, P. A. (1973), 'Status transitions of women students, faculty and administration', in A. S. Rossi and A. Calderwood, *Academic Women on the Move*, Russell Sage Foundation, New York.

Griffiths, V. (1977), 'Sex roles in the secondary school: problems of implementing change', paper read to 'Teaching Girls to be Women' conference, University of Essex, April.

Guardian (1977a), 'University applicants increase', 4 February.

Guardian (1977b), 'Sex discrimination at Institute', 28 February.

Guardian (1977c), 'Education shrouded in green mist', 22 July.

Gurney-Dixon Report (1954), *Early Leaving*, HMSO.

Halmos, P. (1970), *The Choice of Work Areas of Teachers*, Sociological Review Monograph, University of Keele.

Hammersley, M. and Woods, P. (1976), *The Process of Schooling*, Routledge & Kegan Paul, London.

Hannam, C., Smith, P. and Stephenson, N. (1976), *The First Year of Teaching*, Penguin, Harmondsworth.

Hargreaves, D. H. (1967), *Social Relations in a Secondary School*, Routledge & Kegan Paul, London.

Harris, A. S. (1970), *The Second Sex in Academe*, AAUP Bulletin, vol. 3, no. 56.

Harrison, B. G. (1974), *Unlearning the lie: Sexism in the School*, William Morrow, New York.

Hellawall, D. and Smithers, A. (1973–4), 'Commitment to teaching of postgraduate and college-trained students', *National Foundation for Educational Research*, vol. 16, no. 4, pp. 46–51.

Hencke, D. (1976), 'Schools action demanded to save identity', *Guardian*, 9 October.

Hencke, D. (1977a), 'Arts to go under science', *Guardian*, 9 February.

Hencke, D. (1977b), 'Old boy network claim on university posts', *Guardian*, 21 May.

Hencke, D. (1977c), 'The rise, and rise of the Government's "job machine" ', *Guardian*, 7 November.

Hextall, I. (1977), 'The DES and the core curriculum', paper read to BSA Sociology of Education Study group, University of Leicester, February.

Hochschild, A. R. (1973), 'Sex role research', in J. Huber, *Changing Women in a Changing Society*, University of Chicago Press.

Hoyle, E. (1969), *The Role of the Teacher*, Routledge & Kegan Paul, London.

Hudson, L. (1966), *Contrary Imaginations*, Methuen, London.

Hussain, A. (1976), 'The economy and the educational system in capitalist societies', *Economy and Society*, vol. 5, no. 4, pp. 413–34.

Jackson, B. (1962), *Streaming: An education system in miniature*, Routledge & Kegan Paul, London.

Jencks, C. (1975), *Inequality*, Penguin, Harmondsworth.

Jenkins, D. and Shipman, M. D. (1976), *Curriculum: an Introduction*, Open Books, London.

Judd, J. (1977), 'A woman's place is less and less in teaching', *Times Higher Education Supplement*, 19 August, p. 4.

Kamm, J. (1965), *Hope Deferred*, Methuen, London.

Karpf, A. (1977), 'Union dues', *Guardian*, 9 November.

Keddie, N. (1971), 'Classroom knowledge', in M. F. D. Young, *Knowledge and Control*, Macmillan, London.

Keddie, N. (1974), *Tinker, Tailor: the Myth of Cultural Deprivation*, Penguin, Harmondsworth.

Kelsall, R. K. and Kelsall, H. M. (1969), *The School Teacher in England and the United States*, Pergamon, Oxford.

Kerr, J. F. (1968), *Changing the Curriculum*, University of London Press.

Kerr, J. F. (1971), 'The problem of curriculum reform', in R. Hooper, *The Curriculum: Context, Design and Development*, Oliver & Boyd, Edinburgh.

King, W. H. (1965), 'Experimental evidence on comparative attainment in mathematics in single sex and co-educational secondary schools', *Educational Research*, vol. 8.

Klein, V. (1946), *The Feminine Character*, Routledge & Kegan Paul, London.

Knight, L. (1977), 'Flight from home rule', *Guardian*, 24 June.

Kohlberg, L. (1966), 'A cognitive-developmental analysis of children's sex-role concepts and attitudes', in E. Maccoby, *The Development of Sex Differences*, Stanford University Press, California.

Komarovsky, M. (1973), 'Cultural contradictions and sex roles', in J. Huber, *Changing Women in a Changing Society*, University of Chicago Press.

Lacey, C. (1970), *Hightown Grammar*, Manchester University Press.

Lambert, A. (1976), 'The Sisterhood', in Hammersley and Woods (1976), op. cit.

Laslett, P. (1965), *The World We Have Lost*, Charles Scribner's Sons, New York.

Lawson, J. E. and Silver, H. (1973), *A Social History of Education*, Methuen, London.

Lawton, D. (1975), *Class, Culture and the Curriculum*, Routledge & Kegan Paul, London.

Leggatt, T. (1970), 'Teaching as a profession', in J. A. Jackson, *Professions and Professionalization*, Cambridge University Press.

Llewellyn, M. (1977), 'Girls at school', paper read to BSA Sexual Divisions study group, Lanchester Polytechnic, June.

Lobban, G. (1976), 'Sex roles in reading schemes', in Children's Rights Workshop (1976), op. cit.

Lowndes, G. A. (1969), *The Silent Social Revolution*, Oxford University Press.

Lunn, J. C. (1970), *Streaming in the Primary School*, National Foundation for Educational Research, Slough.

Maccoby, E. (1966), *The Development of Sex Differences*, University of Stanford Press, California.

Maccoby, E. (1972), 'Sex differences in intellectual functioning', in Anderson (1972), op. cit.

McCreath, M. (1970), 'Factors influencing choice of higher education', Proceedings of the Sixth Annual Conference of the Society for Research into Higher Education.

McDonald, O. (1976), 'Don's Diary', *Times Higher Educational Supplement*, 14 May.

McIntosh, N. (1975), 'Women and the Open University', in University of

London Teaching Methods Unit Conference Proceedings, *Women in Higher Education*.

Mackie, L. (1977), 'All men – and women – are still not equal', *Guardian*, 3 June.

Mackie, L. and Patullo, P. (1977), *Women at Work*, Tavistock, London.

McRobbie, A. (1977), 'Working class girls' culture', paper read to BSA Sexual Divisions study group, Lanchester Polytechnic, June.

McRobbie, A. and Garber, J. (1976), 'Girls and sub-cultures', in S. Hall and T. Jefferson (1976), *Resistance Through Rituals*, Hutchinson, London.

Manzer, R. A. (1970), *Teachers and Politics*, Manchester University Press.

Marks, P. (1976), 'Femininity in the classroom', in J. Mitchell and A. Oakley, *The Rights and Wrongs of Women*, Penguin, 1976.

Martin, M. K. and Voorhies, B. (1975), *Female of the Species*, Columbia University Press.

Mead, M. (1962), *Male and Female*, Penguin, Harmondsworth.

Midwinter, E. (1972), *Priority Education*, Penguin, Harmondsworth.

Miller, P. McC. and Dale, R. R. (1974), 'A comparison of the degree results of university students from co-educational and single-sex schools', *British Journal of Educational Psychology*, vol. 44, pp. 307-8.

Mitchell, J. (1971), *Women's Estate*, Penguin, Harmondsworth.

Mitchell, J. and Oakley, A. (1976), *The Rights and Wrongs of Women*, Penguin, Harmondsworth.

Moodie, G. C. and Eustace, R. (1974), *Power and Authority in British Universities*, Allen & Unwin, London.

Moody, E. (1968), 'Right in front of everybody', *New Society*, 26 December, pp. 952-3.

Morris, J. (1975), *Conundrum*, Signet, New York.

Morrison, A. and McIntyre, D. (1969), *Teachers and Teaching*, Penguin, Harmondsworth.

Musgrove, F. (1971), *Patterns of Power and Authority in English Education*, Routledge & Kegan Paul, London.

Musgrove, F. and Taylor, P. H. (1969), *Society and the Teacher's Role*, Routledge & Kegan Paul, London.

Newson, J. and Newson, E. (1963), *Patterns of Infant Care in an Urban Community*, Allen & Unwin, London.

Newson, J. and Newson, E. (1968), *Four Years Old in an Urban Community*, Allen & Unwin, London.

Newson, J. and Newson, E. (1976), *Seven Years Old in the Home Environment*, Allen & Unwin, London.

Norris, J. (1977), 'Part-time teachers', *Women and Education*, no. 11, Summer, pp. 3-4.

Oakley, A. (1976), *Housewife*, Penguin, Harmondsworth.

Ormerod, M. B. (1971), 'The social implications factor in attitudes to science', *British Journal of Educational Psychology*, vol. 41, pp. 335-8.

Ormerod, M. B. (1975), 'Subject preference and choice in co-educational and single-sex secondary schools', *British Journal of Educational Psychology*, vol. 45, pp. 257-67.

Parry, J. and Parry, N. (1974), 'The teachers and professionalism; the failure of an occupational strategy', in M. Flude and J. Ahier, *Educability, Schools and Ideology*, Croom-Helm, London.

Phillips, C. (1969), *Changes in Subject Choice at School and University*, Weidenfeld & Nicolson, London.

Pollard, M. (1974), *The Teachers*, Eastland Press, Lavenham, Suffolk.

Poulantzas, N. (1975), *Classes in Contemporary Capitalism*, New Left Books, London.

Rapoport, R. and Rapoport, R. N. (1976), *Dual Career Families Re-examined*, Martin Robertson, London.

Reiter, R. R. (1975), *Toward an Anthropology of Women*, Monthly Review Press, New York.

Richardson, E. (1973), *The Teacher, the School and the Task of Management*, Heinemann, London.

Rosaldo, M. Z. and Lamphere, L. (1974), *Woman, Culture and Society*, Stanford University Press, California.

Rowbotham, S. (1972), *Women, Resistance and Revolution*, Allen Lane, Harmondsworth.

Roy, W. (1968), *The Teachers Union*, Schoolmaster Publishing Co., London.

Rubenstein, D. and Simon, B. (1969), *The Evolution of the Comprehensive School*, Routledge & Kegan Paul, London.

Samuel, J. (1976), 'Women and science', in *Women and Education*, no. 7, p. 5.

Sandgren, L. (1977), *Diversification of Tertiary Education in Sweden*, Stockholm.

Scott, H. (1976), *Women and Socialism*, Alison & Busby, London.

Scott, M. (1977), 'Jobs for the girls', *Guardian*, 9 June.

Secombe, W. (1974), 'The housewife and her labour under capitalism', *New Left Review*, no. 83, pp. 3-24.

Sharpe, S. (1976), *Just Like a Girl*, Penguin, Harmondsworth.

Shaw, J. (1976), 'Finishing school — some implications of sex-segregated education', in Barker and Allen (1976b).

Shepherd, A. (1970-1), 'Married women teachers — the perception and career patterns', *Educational Research*, vol. 13, pp. 191-7.

Shortridge, K. (1970), 'Women as university nigger', *Daily Magazine*, University of Michigan, Ann Arbor, 12 April.

Silver, H. (1973), *Equal Opportunity in Education*, Methuen, London.

Simpson, J. H. and Simpson, R. L. (1969), 'Women and bureaucracy in the semi-professions', in A. Etzioni, *Semi-Professions and their Organization*, Free Press, New York.

Slee, F. W. (1968), 'The feminine image factor of girls' attitudes to school subjects', *British Journal of Educational Psychology*, vol. 38, pp. 212–14.

Smith, C. (1973), 'Adolescence', in M. Smith, S. Parker and C. Smith, *Leisure and Society in Britain*, Allen Lane, Harmondsworth.

Smith, R. (1976), 'Sex and occupational role in Fleet Street', in Barker and Allen (1976a).

Stéhelin, L. (1976), 'Sciences, Women and Ideology', in H. Rose and S. Rose, *The Radicalisation of Science*, Macmillan, London.

Stenhouse, L. (1967), *Culture and Education*, Nelson, London.

Sturt, M. (1967), *The Education of the People*, Routledge & Kegan Paul, London.

Szymanski, A. (1976), 'The Socialization of women's oppression: A Marxist Theory of the changing position of women in Advanced Capitalist Society', *Insurgent Sociologist*, vol. 6, no. 11, Winter.

Taylor, A. J. P. (1965), *British History 1914–1945*, Oxford University Press.

Taylor, W. (1969), *Society and the Training of Teachers*, Faber & Faber, London.

Terman, L. M. and Miles, C. C. (1936), *Sex and Personality*, summarized in Klein, V. (1946), op. cit.

Thompson, D. (1976), 'Women and nineteenth century radical politics', in Mitchell and Oakley (1976), op. cit.

Thompson, H. (1903), *The Mental Traits of Sex*, summarized in Klein (1946), op. cit.

Tiger, L. and Shepher, J. (1977), *Women in the Kibbutz*, Penguin, Harmondsworth.

Times Higher Educational Supplement 1977, 'Not yet a woman's world', 19 August.

Tobach, E. (1972), 'Some evolutionary aspects of human gender', in H. Wortis and C. Rabinowitz, *The Women's Movement*, John Wiley, New York.

Tropp, A. (1957), *The School Teachers*, Heinemann, London.

Turner, B. (1974), *Equality for Some*, Ward Lock Educational, London.

Vallance, E. (1974), 'Hiding the hidden curriculum: an interpretation of the language of justification in nineteenth century educational reform', *Curriculum Theory Network*, vol. 4, no. 1, pp. 13–14.

Webb, D. (1974), 'The Young Sociologist's entry to the Academic World', *British Journal of Sociology*, vol. 25, June, pp. 201–14.

Webb, D. (1977), 'Women in sociology', paper read to BSA Sexual Divisions Study Group, University of Sheffield, April.

Weitz, S. (1977), *Sex Roles*, Oxford University Press, New York.

Bibliography

Whitehead, A. (1976), 'Sexual antagonism in Herefordshire', in Barker and Allen (1976b), op. cit.

Williams, G. *et al.* (1974), *The Academic Labour Market*, Elsevier Scientific Publishing, Amsterdam.

Williams, R. (1965), *The Long Revolution*, Penguin, Harmondsworth.

Willis, P. (1977), *Learning to Labour*, Saxon House, Farnborough.

Wober, M. (1970-1), 'The meanings of convergence and divergence, with data from girls' secondary schools', *Educational Review*, vol. 23, pp. 33-49.

Wolff, J. (1977), 'Women's Studies and Sociology', *Sociology*, vol. 11, no. 1, January, pp. 155-61.

Wolpe, A.-M. (1976), 'The official ideology of education for girls', in M. Flude and J. Ahier, *Educability, Schools and Ideology*, Croom-Helm, London.

Wolpe, A.-M. (1977), *Some Processes in Sexist Education*, Women's Research and Resources Centre, 27 Clerkenwell Close, London, EC1.

Women and Education (1977), 'The EOC and education', no. 10, pp. 10-11, 29 Corkland Road, Chorlton, Manchester 21.

Woods, P. (1976), 'The Myth of Subject Choice', *British Journal of Sociology*, no. 2, June, pp. 130-149.

Woods, P. and Hammersley, M. (1977), *School Experience*, Croom-Helm, London.

Young, M. F. D. (1971), *Knowledge and Control*, Macmillan, London.

Zeigler, H. (1967), *The Political Life of American Teachers*, Prentice-Hall, Englewood Cliffs, New Jersey.

Index

Index

166

Index

social change, desirability for women, 127, 140–141
socialist societies, position of women, 133–5, 137–9
State, role in education, 2–3, 10
Stenhouse, L., 22
student politics, involvement of women, 97
students, women, 93–7; barriers to women becoming, 85–90
Sturt, M., 7
Suffragette Movement, 14, 18, 20
Sweden, educational policies, 133–4; housing policy and socialization of housework, 139
Szymanski, A., 136

Taunton Commission, 1868, on education of girls in endowed schools, 7
Taylor, A.J.P., 85
Taylor, W., 120
teacher training, cutbacks, 120, 128; nineteenth century, 7–8, 86, 117–119; opportunities for women in, 86–7; twentieth century, 86–7, 119–121
teaching, commitment of women teachers, 115–17; part-time, disadvantages of, 114; special roles of women in, 110–112, 121–3; wastage rate of women in, 116–117; women in, 74, 108–26
Teeny-Bopper culture, 36–7
Terman, L.M. and Miles, C.C., 26
textbooks, sexism in, 24
Thompson, H., 26
Training Services Agency, 72, 128
Turner, B., 9

UCCA, report on admission of women to university in 1976, 91

unemployment, 10, 15, 72–3, 128–9; consequences for women, 19, 69, 72–3, 128–9; of school leavers, 72–3, 128–9
uniform, school, 41, 47
unions, participation of women in, 123–5, 136; teaching, 123–5; women as members, 123–5, 136
universities, opportunities for women, 12–13, 83–90; power structures, 104–5; women lecturers, 100–105; women students, 12–13, 90, 93–7

Vallance, E., 47
verbal skills, girls', 26–8, 29, 31, 53, 70
votes, for women, 14

Webb, D., 96, 100
Whitehead, A., 105
Williams, Raymond, 21
Willis, Paul, 131–2
Wilson, Harold, 63
Wolpe, A.M., 25, 41, 47–8, 49–50
Women's Liberation Movement, 1, 42, 125, 130
Women's Studies, aims of, 42, 97, 98–9; content of, 42, 44, 97, 98–9; growth, 42, 44, 97
working class girls, culture of, 35–8; education of, 3, 6, 7, 8, 10–11, 16, 51, 60, 65

young children, sex-stereotyping in upbringing, 23–6, 29–34; teaching as a feminine activity, 110–12

Zeigler, H., 124